Praise for ASYLUM

"Judy Bolton-Fasman's *Asylum* is a masterfully written and compelling memoir, sparkling with love, mystery, humor, and wonder. Delving into family secrets, Bolton-Fasman illuminates a critical period in American Cold War history. Seldom have I felt so moved by the complexities of a family story told with such intelligence and warmth."
—**Helen Fremont**, author of *The Escape Artist*
and *After Long Silence: A Memoir*

"*Asylum*, Judy Bolton-Fasman's fascinating memoir, is populated by vivid, complex, and original characters, from whom the writer inherited two languages and several mysteries to unravel and contradictory stories to set straight. . . . *Asylum* addresses the untold story of Jewish immigration from Cuba, twentieth-century American history, and family conflict, but as a kind of detective story begun by Bolton-Fasman as a little girl and completed after years of research and reflection. It's a delightful page-turner."
—**Anita Diamant**, author of *The Red Tent* and *Boston Girl*

"*Asylum* has enough passion, family secrets, and political intrigue to keep even the most jaded memoir reader on the edge of his seat. But what carried me along was the warmth, precision, and gentle humor of Judy Bolton-Fasman's writing. Hers is a voice that charms and captures you from the opening paragraphs."
—**Stephen McCauley**, author of *The Object of My Affection*
and the upcoming *My Ex-Life*

"True to her name, Judy Bolton-Fasman is a brilliant detective, searching for answers about her father both in the world and in her own heart. This book is true to its name, as well, ultimately offering the solace the word "Asylum" suggests. A stunning meditation on grief and secrets—finely observed, beautifully written."
—**Gayle Brandeis**, author of *The Art of Misdiagnosis:*
Surviving My Mother's Suicide

"Most children are spies, trying to uncover and decipher clues as to who their parents really are. But very few children discover their *parents* are spies. Real spies. In *Asylum*, Judy Bolton-Fasman proves herself to be the cleverest, most perceptive, and most compassionate of detectives, solving the mystery of her father's secret life in South America and her parents' troubled marriage. A deeply moving, beautifully written, original story of family and faith, passion and mourning, betrayal, and love."
—**Eileen Pollack**, author of *A Perfect Life* and
The Only Woman in the Room: Why Science Is Still a Boy's Club

"A common optical illusion of childhood is that your parents are exactly who you assume them to be. But even as a young girl, Judy Bolton-Fasman sensed that her father had a hidden life. A tender investigation into her own detective work as a girl builds into a profound investigation of family secrets, memory, and the legacy of being the daughter of a spy."
—**Howard Axelrod**, author of *The Point of Vanishing:*
A Memoir of Two Years of Solitude

"*Asylum* is a deeply moving memoir that investigates the ever-complicated knot of familial love, loss and longing.
Judy Bolton-Fasman beautifully captures that urge so many of us have to better understand those loved ones who were close to us yet nonetheless eluded our grasp."
—**Tova Mirvis**, author of *Visible City*
and *The Book of Separation: A Memoir*

"Judy Bolton-Fasman's profound quest to understand the mystery surrounding her Sephardic Cuban mother and her Ashkenazi American father is immensely moving, showing how unmasking hurt can lead to healing and finding the asylum of a wide open heart. An unforgettable, deeply spiritual, culturally rich memoir!"
—**Ruth Behar**, author of *Lucky Broken Girl* and *Letters from Cuba*

ASYLUM

ASYLUM

A MEMOIR OF FAMILY SECRETS

JUDY BOLTON-FASMAN

[M]

MANDEL VILAR PRESS

This book is typeset in Kepler Std 11/15. The paper used in this book meets the minimum requirements of ANSI/NISO Z39.48-1992 (R1997). ∞

Designed by Sophie Appel

All images in this book are courtesy of the author.

Author's note: *Asylum* recounts my story as I remember it. As I strive to retrieve my memories to represent my truth, the timeline remains deliberately nonlinear. I have blurred some places and changed some names to shield the identities of those whose privacy merits protection.

Parts of this book appeared previously in the following publications: "Letter of Last Resort" in *Modern Loss*; "Trastienda" in *Off Assignment*; "Not Even a Glass of Water" in *Cleaver Magazine*; "Judy Bolton, Girl Detective, Girl Thief" in *Lunch Ticket*; "Heathen, Slave, Woman" in *Brevity Magazine*; "Reciting Kaddish as a Daughter" in *The Forward*; "The Ninety Day Wonder" in *Rappahannock Review*; "With Love From Harold: A Father's War Story Offers Hope in an Uncertain Time" in *Cognoscenti*; "The Spy Who Loved Me" in *Cognoscenti*; "The Somnambulist" in *Thimble Literary Magazine*; "The First Anniversary of the Pandemic" in *Exquisite Pandemic*. The author holds the copyright to these articles.

Publisher's Cataloging-in-Publication Data

Name: Bolton-Fasman, Judy, Author

Title: Asylum: A Memoir of Family Secrets

Description: Simsbury, Connecticut, Mandel Vilar Press [2021]

Identifiers: ISBN 978-1942134-770 (pbk.)
E-ISBN: 978-1942134-787 (ebook)

Subjects: LCSHL Bolton-Fasman, Judy Memoir / Jewish Sephardic and Ashkenazi/ United States and Cuba / Latinx / Detective Story of Family Secrets and Mysteries/ American Cold War History

Classification LCC PS 3569 B3387 Z46 2021

Printed in the United States of America

21 22 23 24 25 26 27 28 29 / 9 8 7 6 5 4 3 2 1

Mandel Vilar Press
19 Oxford Court, Simsbury, Connecticut 06070
www.americasforconservation.org | www.mvpublishers.org

To My Past—K. Harold Bolton z'l and Matilde A. Bolton

To My Present—Ken Fasman

To My Future—Anna Fasman and Adam Fasman

There is no greater agony than bearing an untold story inside of you.
—Maya Angelou

Turn it and turn it again, for everything is in it.
—Ethics of Our Fathers

Each of us has a name, given to us by God,
and given to us by our father and mother.
—Zelda (Israeli poet)

CONTENTS

PART III

Burn This

There is a Jewish saying that an uninterpreted dream is like an unopened letter from God—a letter that surely must contain secrets of the universe.

The only letters I received that muggy summer when I stayed on the non-air-conditioned side of the 92nd Street Y were from my father, usually cheery cards ("Well, hello over there!"), or thin sheets of yellow legal-pad paper with bits of curmudgeonly wisdom designed to steer my focus away from my recent heartbreak: "You're a smart kid—you can do this! You can finish that darn thesis! Don't let all that time and money be for naught!"

This time was different. In my mail was an unusually thick envelope that bore the return address of my father's Hartford office. I knew he had more on his mind than usual that summer, and the heavily taped envelope with too much postage signaled as much. It came on the heels of another letter he had sent, his more typical one-page kind, telling me, "I shall no longer pay the reservation fee at your school."

During the summer of 1985, I commuted on the Madison Avenue bus to the computer lab at Columbia, where I struggled to finish a collection of short stories for my MFA. It was also the summer my heart shattered into a million jagged pieces when my boyfriend vanished, as if our eight years together had never happened. My loneliness—or, as my father put it, "lonesomeness"—not only saddened him; it magnified his own feeling of aloneness in the world.

My father was not one for phone calls. After the initial "How are you's," he was all breathing and silence, so he had taken to writing me a couple of times a week. His postscript was always the same: "Write to me at the office. I don't want your mother to know that we're corresponding." We both knew my mother would be wildly suspicious were she not included in our correspondence.

While my father was a reluctant talker under the best of circumstances, he was a formal, old-fashioned writer who used words like "shan't" and "cheers" and "salutations." He always signed his cards and notes to me, "Your Father." Love was not in his vocabulary.

Did he love me? I knew he worried about me. I was the sensitive firstborn daughter who was the frequent target of her mother's hair-trigger moods. His worry was love. But I sensed this latest correspondence, massive as it was, would reflect that he was older, more tired, and showing more overt signs of his Parkinson's disease. He had already grumbled that my mother "was getting more difficult to tolerate," finally defeating him with her relative youth—she was seventeen years younger—and with her epic tantrums and fiercely won economic independence.

This time, I was sure he would dispense with his bonhomie, his homespun wisdom, his greetings and salutations, and finally tell me all that I had been yearning to know since my earliest days.

I carried the large envelope carefully to my room as if it were fragile. Addressed in my father's now shaky print, it felt substantial. Weighty. Was it an opus of his life? A compilation of regrets? A decision to divorce my mother at last, along with a laundry list of her failures, her denunciations? Whatever it was, it called for a private place in which to read it.

As I went up the elevator, I trembled with the recognition of yet another possibility—that it contained a suicide note. The letters of my father's hand-printing, once so tall and commanding, had lately begun to droop. My father's printing had been his forte, his identity, and his imprint on the world. It announced that he was a serious, meticulous, determined man. I had always loved and saluted the stalwart letters he formed—one and the same on birthday cards, valentines, and now in the letters he sent me—in honor of the Navy man he once was. But the last time I was home,

I noticed that his left arm shook and he walked with a shuffle. "Leave me alone," he muttered whenever I asked how he was feeling.

What if this letter contained my father's final confession? What if it was a compendium of his *trastiendas*—the word my Cuban mother had adapted as a more resonant way to describe secrets. According to her, every person carries at least one trastienda from a place in the heart where such secrets thrill the day and deepen the night. Perhaps these trastiendas were more like dark thoughts that had been in the cobwebbed corners of his mind? Once I knew about these trastiendas, would it make me like Icarus, flying too close to the sun and dropping from the sky? Would it be like opening Pandora's jar—or, as it was later mistranslated, her box—of woes and releasing them to the world? Reading about my father's troubles in his hand might make them my own. I was afraid to know everything about him. And yet I was too curious to leave his secrets alone.

Trastienda is a Spanish noun that literally means a storage room in the back of a warehouse; I imagine it as a place to stash broken dreams. It is like the small storage room in the basement of my childhood home where orphaned books and bygone art projects were—as my father would say, with his penchant for tried-and-true expressions—put out to pasture.

This letter might be telling me that my father no longer had dreams to comfort him. After all, a trastienda is a dark, dank place, and this letter carried a whiff of that because no one's trastiendas were more hidden away than those of my parents. If my father were to confess his, surely it would be in a missive as large and securely bound as this one.

Secrets had always saturated the air in the house. They rustled in drawers, were stashed in closets, often alluded to yet never spoken. I felt them, stumbled over them. "*Secreticos, secreticos, secreticos,*" my mother said—a dire, if vague, warning.

There was one more possibility for my father's letter. He may have meant it to function as a Letter of Last Resort—a note the British prime minister writes out four times for each Royal Navy submarine carrying Trident nuclear missiles. My father, a former United States Naval officer and admirer of Winston Churchill, would certainly relate to the concept. The prime minister personally seals the Letter of Last Resort. The only person thereafter allowed to open it is the commander of one of the four submarines, and only following a nuclear attack on Great Britain in which the prime minister and second-in-command are already con- firmed dead. The letter contains the prime minister's instructions on what to do going forward: retaliate and risk more lives, or leave intact whatever humanity has survived.

My father respected a chain of command. In our particular chain, I was his survivor; I was the commander of the family warship should all else fail. Perhaps he intended for me to open his letter and know his tras- tiendas when the time was right, and perhaps that time was now.

In my room, the red light on my answering machine throbbed, insis- tent. I thought for a moment it might be the ex-boyfriend, come to beg forgiveness. I hit play.

"Listen," came my father's voice, which had become low and gravelly from the Parkinson's, "I sent you a letter that should have arrived today. I hope to God you're hearing this before you open it. Do not read it. In fact, I need you to burn it."

His voice had the same underlying panic as when he would come home from his accountant's job and take me aside to whisper: "What kind of mood is your mother in?" The answer was never good.

Burn it? But this was the letter I had been waiting for. The confession. The explanation. The spilling of all the secrets that had shrouded my childhood. The key, the clue. The one final piece of the puzzle. Burn it?

I held my father's letter up to the fluorescent light to catch a faint glimpse of its contents. All I saw was the X-ray outline of folded, lined sheets full of scribbling—the crabbed, crowded letters another sign of Parkinson's.

Back when Harold Bolton was stronger and more intense, his was the terrifying voice on the other side of the bathroom door shouting: "Navy shower! Rinse. Turn the water off. Soap up. Rinse again. Too much water goes to waste in this house!" Naked, shivering, embarrassed, I did as he commanded. When it came to my father, obedience had always prevailed.

But it was more than obedience that brought me, reluctantly, to the battered gray metal desk in my room, where I took out a lighter, a vestige of a smoking habit I had mostly kicked. I had flicked the same lighter on and off a few months before when I burned pages of my journal; I couldn't stand the possibility that someone might read about my neediness, my depression, my own thoughts of suicide.

That afternoon in my nine-by-eleven-foot room, fear doused the curiosity vested in me by my name: Judy Bolton, Girl Detective. I would not solve this one last mystery, the greatest mystery of my life, after all.

I placed the lighter close to the envelope, until the blue-rimmed orange flame caught a small, flattened corner. From there, the fire spread quickly. This was my summer of constant panic, and now anxiety pushed me to set my father's words aflame. No apartment, no degree, no boyfriend. No answers. If I opened the envelope, I would come face to face with secrets I was still too afraid to learn. I was years away from understanding that I could work purposefully, deliberately, against the *ataque de nervios* that was always lurking. Like my mother, I felt as if I were a nerve away from a complete breakdown.

In the end, I destroyed the divine trastiendas I was sure were in that letter—trastiendas that had the power to crack open the sky. I dropped the burning letter, sealed and intact, into the metal garbage can, and watched it disintegrate into ash. A raised bald-eagle stamp remained distinct and resolute until it was finally a different, unrecognizable form of matter.

Part I

CHAPTER I

Judy Bolton, Girl Detective

I was six years old the first time I saw my name along the spine of a mystery novel on my cousin's bookshelf: Judy Bolton. The thrill of seeing it there, emblazoned on a book, never got old for me.

I am a Judy. Except in legal documents, I have never been a Judith. Judy Bolton was a well-known fictional detective in the 1930s and '40s: the "Girl Detective," never quite as popular as Nancy Drew but second to none when it came to solving mysteries. And there was one great, essential mystery that I, Judy Bolton, had always wanted to solve: the mystery of my parents.

K. Harold Bolton was older and commanding, a Yale grad, a military man who didn't settle into marriage and family until the age of forty, and then to a woman seventeen years his junior. My first memory of my father was the towering view I had of him from my stroller. He was a silent presence but, like sensing the wind, I knew he was there.

He was an accountant, with an office in Hartford, Connecticut—although I sometimes heard the sound of his rapid-fire adding machine emanating from our basement during tax season. Why he chose accounting as a profession was its own mystery, as he seemed unable to keep track of the family expenses, despite drawing up ultimately-useless household budgets on pieces of shiny white cardboard that came with his freshly pressed shirts. My grandfather, a civil engineer, sent his son a steady succession of letters full of optimism and financial advice.

My mother, the former Matilde Alboukrek, left Cuba at age twenty-two, with little more than a few photos, and memories that sounded too good to be true. She was a beauty queen, afraid that her good looks were fading, and also a master linguist, with knowledge of at least five languages.

I was the only kid whose mother walked her to and from school. One day when the entire class had to stay late, she tired of waiting, so she lugged my brother in his stroller to the second floor and opened the classroom door without a knock as if it were her own house. She spoke loudly, breathlessly, in a café Cubano accent. "*Que pasa con esta vieja fea?*" she said, confident that no one understood what she was saying as she wondered what was wrong with my "old and ugly" homeroom teacher. My mother's foreignness forever separated me from the rest of the class, and from that day forward, they called me the Spic 'n' Span baby.

Oddly, though, I was unable to hear what the others claimed they heard when my mother sang the birthday song as "*Chapee Bersday to Joo.*" I had willed myself into a self-protective deafness in which I could not discern her accent at all.

Those were the facts about my parents. Still, I always knew, or at least believed, that something was missing, or wrong. Something unspoken. My parents were an accumulation of random details that mostly pointed in diverging directions: culture, nationality, age. They were of two worlds; therefore, I was of two worlds. Their union made them unique and, ultimately, incomprehensible. Like the household budget, their stories never added up.

True to my detective heritage, I wanted to know them, even more than most of the kids I knew wanted to know their parents. I *had* to reconcile their stories. I *had* to reconcile them in my mind as a couple, and as my father and my mother. They were exotic, mismatched, yet perfectly matched. I needed to get to the bottom of the murky story of how they eventually married. They activated a curiosity and a need to build a world that made sense to me.

My father was the healer in the family, taking care of all manner of cuts and splinters and colds. When I was little I was so desperate to be like him that I one time took his razor and shaved my face, just as I'd seen him do. Among the sweetest times we had together was when I watched him take a razor to the white foamy shaving-cream-covered beard on his face. I quickly discovered that I was not so thick-skinned as he when I accidentally sliced the side of my chin, my blood mixing with his menthol-scented shaving cream. I screamed, which left me no time to hide the evidence of the bloodied blade before my parents rushed into the bathroom and saw what I had done.

"*Por qué?*" my mother said with anger and disappointment in her voice. "Why would you shave your face instead of your legs like me?"

"I wanted to be like Daddy," I sobbed. This inflamed her even more.

"*No le digas a nadie que hiciste!*" she said. Don't tell anyone what you did. "Tell them you ran into a sharp corner of the bookcase!"

"We should take her for stitches," my father said as he applied a stinging styptic pencil to stanch the blood.

"Not on her face. She'll look like a *monstruo*."

Eventually I healed naturally and the two scars that remained looked as if a monstruo had taken two small bites out of me.

My parents. I loved them. I hated them.

My father wore weighty brown and white wing-tip Oxfords to work, his footfalls tapping out an idiosyncratic Morse code on the stairs that signaled he'd hold me accountable for the educational television show I didn't watch, the enlightening book I didn't read, the fresh air I wasn't getting.

Even as a child, I knew he had lived an entire life before he met and married my mother, but he protected his past like a secret love, driving me to want to know as much as I could about him. Photos were scant. Who and where had he been during that time between Yale and his inexplicable choice of wife?

As a child, I would follow him around the house. He knew things. He solved things. With him, an ordinary household task like bleeding the radiators took on the gravity of a wartime mission. He wore safety glasses—round, non-prescription lenses with silver wire mesh on the side to protect his eyes further—and arrayed the screwdrivers that would induce the telltale whoosh of a radiator gone bone-dry. He caught the water in a drinking glass from which I sipped one time, wanting to see what "the dregs of winter" tasted like. They tasted metallic and cloudy. "Too curious for your own good," he said, shaking his head. "Curiosity killed the cat."

And yet he named me after a fictional heroine whose chief attribute was her curiosity.

My mother resisted the name Judith to the last. It was one of their earliest tussles, whether to name me after a living or dead relative. In Matilde's Cuban Sephardic world, it was the living, always the living, that mattered. My square-jawed, all-American Connecticut father, otherwise an atheist, adhered nevertheless to the Ashkenazic custom of naming babies after dead relatives. For Dad, it was what the dead had accomplished that counted.

In my mother's tightly-knit matriarchy, the eldest daughter always took the name of the mother, or her mother, which put me in line to become a Matilde, like my mom, or an Elisa, like my *abuela*, grandmother. But it was my father's mother who helped swing the vote by insisting that it might very well kill her if I were named after a living, breathing person.

And so, the *J* in Judith and the *F* in Frances stood for the initials of my father's favorite cousin and mentor, the late James Frederic Rosen— Jimmy—but my dad was a reader of dime-story crime novels and certainly knew of the Girl Detective who solved mysteries for the good of the world. I would come to feel that, with my name, he had given me a special mission.

From the beginning they called me Judy, never Judith. Judy Bolton. My father, after all, had shortened his own name: Kenneth Harold was forever known as Harold and, in a pinch, K. Harold. He never sliced his first name to a Ken or popularized it to a backslapping Kenny. Unlike its counterpart *C*, the letter *K* was unambiguously hard, ramrod straight on one side, the perfect letter to lean on. A letter from which to fly the flag that my dad revered, the Stars and Stripes that he flew from his bedroom on every national holiday. The flag that would drape his coffin. Dad's leather luggage, his chunky signet ring, and the check register as big as a ledger book were all monogrammed with an indelible *K*. I grew up in the shadow of that *K*—a patch of darkness that was meant to cultivate good posture, impeccable manners, and fair outcomes.

Even before I learned of the Girl Detective from the spine of that book on a cousin's shelf, I attempted to solve little mysteries through searching, snooping, imagining, and even through praying. No matter that curiosity killed the cat. No matter that Jimmy, the relative I never knew, was a prankster who managed to poke his left eye out on a tree branch as a kid. Even the possibility of death—which I didn't understand at that age, anyway—did not deter me. I couldn't help myself. I came by my inquisitiveness honestly through a name that reflected my father's unspoken hopes and concerns for me.

But that was not quite how I wound up using my legacy. Instead, I created my own clues, only to wow people in a show of deciphering them. Fictional Judy Bolton spied for the good of her family and community, but mine was a darker brand of sleuthing. Unlike her—and unlike her rival, Nancy Drew, who drove a spiffy blue roadster and had a perfect boyfriend—I worked hard to create and solve my own tangle of loose ends, bandit and detective rolled into one.

Fictional Judy's cases were tied up in neat endings. My childhood investigations were scavenger hunts, during which I stole objects that I craved: plastic calculators at school that showed off black and white buttons with red numbers. Books from the library about latchkey kids that I swiped to somehow prepare myself for war or destruction, or my parents' possible divorce, or loneliness.

Above all, I loved the irresistible shiny bracelets and rings that my classmates showed off and then carelessly stashed in their cubbies and desks. I slunk and sneaked at the Edward Morley School in West Hartford, an elementary school that was heavily populated with pretty Nancy Drews. I was jealous of them, those girls with their shiny hair and, I imagined, equally shiny roadsters. I planted red herrings around the classroom. I was the clever thief who knew what mattered most to my ponytailed classmates, and gladly took it from them. I was the phantom thief who struck after yet another birthday party from which the Nancys had excluded me. I stole from these girls to forget that I was short, chubby, hirsute. I could tolerate their derision because I had their sweet little change purses and hand-knit scarves stuffed in my tin Partridge Family lunchbox.

In a few days, I would return the loot by stashing it in a corner of the coatroom and "finding" it. This made me indispensable to the Nancys, who had fathers who were young and carefree, not seventeen years older than their Cuban wife. They did not have mothers from a place so mysterious that no one was allowed to leave it or visit it. Somehow, coming from Cuba—a country to which we had no access in those days as a family or as Americans—made my mother both volatile and exotic.

The mysteries at school I could create easily and solve quickly. They distracted me, soothed me. The mysteries at home were not so simple.

While confined to my parents' bed with a drug-resistant strep throat, I raised the volume on *As the World Turns* to provide cover for my work of going through their closets and drawers in their room, otherwise filled with the almost unbearable racket of too much stuff in too small a space. I crept over the worn gray carpet, careful not to set off any creaking. I pocketed a fake pearl necklace and matching clip-on earrings from my mother's vanity, really a rickety desk she had transformed with speckled contact paper, gold trim, and crepe skirting. When she panicked that her jewelry was gone—*Donde esta mis arretes!*—I saw to it that the earrings reappeared and that I would be the one to find them. I would be my mother's hero, and for the moment I was safe from her.

In school I searched for what I didn't have, but at home I searched for what I didn't know. Whatever that was, it eluded me, maddeningly. I rummaged through my mother's walk-in closet, an island of eternal twilight and forbidden possibilities, touching the pretty clothes from Lord & Taylor that she hid from my father. ("*Shah*, this is none of your business!") I longed to wear her slender high heels and her sequined dresses, and press my Aunt Gladys's hand-me-down cashmere sweaters against my cheek, where I hoped they would impart their history to me.

The rapturous fuchsia sheath from the Siegel Shop, a tony store in West Hartford Center, presented the very adult possibilities of love and beauty. Throughout the winter that dress hung in the closet swathed in plastic wrapping, waiting for my mother to wear it on the occasion of my uncle José's spring wedding. I was to be the flower girl. Delicately embroidered with roses, the dress fit snuggly over a long slip of a slightly darker hue, with pointy satin shoes dyed to match. I opened the wrapping and slipped both parts of the dress over my pajamas as I toddled in the shoes, stumbling right into my father's arms. I thought he would punish me. Instead, a co-conspirator, he whispered, "Your mother had better not see you in that getup."

The clothing, rustling around me, whispering, still refused to reveal its secrets. Like the yellow linen suit my mother had worn on the eve of her honeymoon. "I paid for that outfit myself. *Me costé!*" It had cost her a large chunk of her final paycheck from the watch factory, where she had spent her time typing invoices and plumping up on pastries. Although she never wore the yellow suit again, to me it conjured fantasies stoked by Doris Day movies and the star-spangled life my mother must have imagined she'd have by becoming Mrs. K. Harold Bolton. That life never materialized. "Your father is the poorest man I know who went to Yale!"

I was determined to go through my father's crowded drawers the same way I rooted around in my mother's forbidden closet. I looked for pictures, matchbooks, scraps of paper with addresses on them so I could invent plausible stories that would fill the gaps of my knowledge about them. I dragged a stepstool from the bathroom to unearth what would help me piece together whatever they weren't telling me. By the time I no longer needed the stool to reach my father's top drawer, I had just begun to understand the intentions behind such discoveries as the package of condoms or the well-thumbed paperback of *Coffee, Tea or Me: The Uninhibited Memoirs of Two Airline Stewardesses.*

In my quest to find the unknowable, I drilled down even further to discover small details in my father's wallet—details stuffed in a billfold thick with dry-cleaning slips and dollar bills. These mundane findings spurred me to do a more complete sweep of the top of his dresser, which felt as crowded as the downtown stores my mother and I visited on Saturday afternoons: a shot glass emblazoned with "Yale 1940," wrapped pieces of Dentyne gum, golf tees, dehydrated snow globes from family vacations that had to be within driving distance for my flying-phobic mother, and outdated calendars from insurance and fuel companies.

I combed through my father's notes and files on the household budget he couldn't balance, reading names and numbers in his orderly, powerful print, looking for clues to where the money my mother said we didn't have went. Words like *MORTAGE* and *HEAT* floated between urgent asterisks. He bundled his canceled checks in used envelopes that looked like something had torn them open with its teeth.

Most magical of all was a heart-shaped box stitched in red and blue, standing out because it was so curiously soft and feminine against my father's mahogany highboy. The box was a souvenir from Guatemala, a place he visited long before he met my mother. I found a picture of him in it labeled "Guatemala 1952." His smile is broad and uncensored. It was hard for me to reconcile the photograph with the quasi-military man I knew. He stands in billowing khakis and a pith helmet, the kind of outfit I had seen on television safaris and that inspired me to imagine him on his own great adventure, perhaps hunting big game. In reality, he was the Americano colonialist. He grabbed that picture out of my hand when he saw I had discovered it.

In the heart-shaped box he kept a silver ring, serious and dense and as declarative as the ring of a monarch. His initials, KHB, were stamped on the ring. I loved to spin it around my middle finger and steal it for the night, keeping it under my pillow as a talisman.

Another photograph, another possible clue, showed my father in a small black and white picture, dated 1941, that he had sent to his mother and sister during the war. On the back he had written, "With Love from Harold." A year out of Yale, he was probably on duty then in the North Atlantic, running guns and butter—food and supplies—to the British in Greenland before America was officially in the war. In the picture he is below deck, where it is dark and windowless; nevertheless, his gaze is dreamy, suggesting that he is happily drifting.

My father never drifted for long. He would read the sky and eventually right himself to know exactly where he was going. During my childhood I only saw my father with that dreamy look when he watched over me at night if I were sick or if the weather outside my window was stormy. What was he gazing at out that window? What did he see? I was jealous of that life he led before me—a life in which he had not foreseen me.

In the Navy snapshot he has lost a lot of weight from compulsory exercise and adrenaline. It looks like he has punched extra holes in his belt. His hat falls below his ears as if from the weight of the brassy naval insignia. His Adam's apple is prominent, his neck muscles taut. There on his left ring finger sits the KHB ring, years away from its place in the heart-shaped box, the only physical link between then and now.

For all the times I stared at the picture, it was only so much later, after my father's death, that I noticed he'd been holding a cigar stub in his left hand. I knew so many things about him so well—his handwriting, the souvenirs, the photographs—and yet I was still missing so much.

In my sleuthing, I investigated all of my father's items, right down to his rack of pipes, silent and stony, as if representing a person who no longer existed. When I flash back to those pipes today I think of the artist Magritte. "This is not a pipe," the Belgian surrealist wrote below his painting of a pipe. It was not a real pipe, only a drawing of one.

This was not my father. My father was a flesh-and-blood man who was not really there. A tourist in magical lands I had never been to, a veteran of a war that took up too much space in his head, a man who kept his memories, forever encoded, in a heart-shaped box. A man who never answered innocent questions about where he went during the war or what the weather was like in Guatemala. "Loose lips sink ships," my World War II father said. I liked the rhyme but didn't understand it. In adulthood, I wondered what massive, destructive secrets he must have kept to himself.

My parents were once so dazzling. On the Saturday nights of my childhood, they dressed in glamour to go out, my father in a navy blazer and gray pleated pants, my mother beginning with a pointy bra and heavy girdle, whose fasteners snapped onto the reinforced tops of shimmery silk stockings. She slipped on a short glittery dress and black boots that looked poured over her legs. *"La mas linda della familia,"* said my besotted father, using his serviceable Spanish with the Connecticut accent. The most beautiful in the family.

When they came home late, I spied through the half-open door to their room as my father pulled off my mother's long black boots. Mom on the bed, dreamy and sleepy, whispering, "Too much dancing."

CHAPTER 2

Shark-Finned Chrysler

I knew from my mother's increasingly embellished bedtime stories that she spent her first year in the United States living in Brooklyn cold-water flats and pacing in acrid subway stations waiting for a train to take her to work. I eagerly anticipated version after version—stories in which Matilde, the self-appointed heroine, endured seasonal cold and intense homesickness, until pneumonia had her quitting night school and staying in bed for a month, feverish and disoriented. In some versions she was inconvenienced; in others, she nearly died. The Hungarian girls she worked with at the watch factory that first year visited with homemade pastries. They had fled their own political conflagration in Budapest three years earlier; Matilde was beginning to watch Castro take over her country. He had come down from the Sierra Maestra Mountains, marching into the center of Havana on January 1, 1959.

"Castro sat with me one time, you know," she told me, the story worn smooth through repetition. "He sat next to me on a bench at the university and invited me for coffee."

"What did you do?" I asked, my eyes shining in anticipation each time.

"I had to say no. He had a handgun peeking out from his jacket."

This odd meeting took place, she said, near the famous staircase at the University of Havana, a wide set of steps that fanned down to the street. My mother always knew how to stage a scene. She had been studying social work at the university over her father's, Abrahan's, objections. "*La universidad* is no place for girls," he said when she first announced her educational plans beyond finishing the Instituto High School in Havana. He berated Abuela for encouraging Matilde to register for classes. "But if she doesn't go to school she'll be a *burra* like me, sewing until her fingers fall off," Elisa cried.

While my father was tight-lipped about his past, I grew up in thrall to my mother's stories, especially the one about the shark-finned yellow Chrysler.

On a stifling August day in 1959, Matilde Alboukrek brought a gift for her friend Violeta's new baby girl. Matilde could barely tamp down her jealousy—a jealousy that, like her eyes, was *verde y claro*, green and clear. The feeling lodged in her throat. Matilde had come to the United States to follow a boy and the boy had abandoned her, leaving her alone in a strange country with jealousy and loneliness her only constants.

Now her story soared back into the past, back to Cuba in the early 1950s, to those same university steps close to where Castro had asked her for coffee. It was on those same steps where Matilde first met Manuel, a towering character in her memory. Manuel was the handsome doctor at the university clinic who dressed her wounds when she fell on the steps and scraped her knee. Three weeks later, the stars aligned and there he was again at the Purim Ball of 1954 in Havana's El Patronato.

There at the ball was the doctor who had dressed her knee. Matilde was wearing a black sleeveless velvet gown that her mother had sewn for her, the neckline studded with tiny rhinestones. It was fated.

They danced all night. Matilde believed in signs and wonders more than she believed in God, so when Manuel left Cuba in 1958 for a residency in New York City, with the idea of eventually becoming a doctor in Israel, Matilde convinced her father that she, too, had to leave the country. "The *comunistas* are overrunning the university," she insisted. "They are trying to recruit me to join the party."

The lovesick Matilde bought herself a ticket to the United States with the money she had saved from her part-time secretarial job with a Zionist organization.

"Why are you here?" Manuel asked her when they met at a diner near Bellevue Hospital in New York.

"There is no future in Cuba," said Matilde.

"For you or for me?"

"For us."

Manuel studied his coffee cup. "I told you in Havana I would be going to Israel. I'm a Zionist," he said.

"So am I."

"Not like me. You wouldn't be able to handle being on a kibbutz. You wear too much makeup. You're terrified of animals. How will you live among dogs and cats and chickens?"

Matilde was forced to rearrange her fairytale. Heartbroken, she tried to make a go of it in Brooklyn without Manuel. She lasted two months. Back in Cuba in 1958, though, she was restless, so she applied for permanent residency in the United States. She returned to New York on July 1, 1959, this time for good.

Her father's cousins David and Sarah encouraged Matilde to go to Saturday night dances for Jewish singles, but Matilde would never admit she was lonely. She pretended to prefer watching *Perry Mason* and *Lawrence Welk*. "Those dances are for *chusmas*," unrefined girls with ankle bracelets and bright red toenail polish on the prowl for men of equally questionable social status. The dances in Brooklyn would never rival the Purim Ball of 1954 when she danced with her doctor. That night she had been among the queen's four attendants—a very high honor for a girl whose father couldn't afford to buy the title of Queen of the Ball.

It was five years after the Purim Ball and just one month after her return to America that Matilde attended Violeta's baby shower, all the while brooding that she, too, should have been married by now, with a home of her own and a baby on the way. Before she could work herself into a fury, all-American Connecticut accountant K. Harold Bolton—older, slim, dashing, distinguished—roared into her life driving a shark-finned yellow Chrysler to Violeta's apartment.

"He's a *caballero*, a gentleman," whispered Violeta. "*Y bien educado.* And he speaks Spanish."

"*Mucho gusto*," said Harold, bending to kiss Matilde's hand. He had a deep tan and close-cropped hair—handsome like Harry Belafonte, she thought.

"*Igualmente*," said Matilde, charmed. "How do you know Spanish?"

"I've traveled in Central America."

On their first date, as Matilde sat with her ginger ale across from her dashing new suitor in a Manhattan bar, she folded her hands in her lap so that he wouldn't notice them shaking.

With sex on hold until marriage, theirs was a whirlwind romance. "Your father took me to everything sports—the Yankees, the Yale Bowl," my mother told me. She was willing to live with Harold's sports fandom. He was, after all, an Americano and a Yale graduate.

Six weeks to the day they met, they were engaged.

Their first wedding was a colorless civil ceremony in the city hall of New Haven, Connecticut, in anticipation of the religious ceremony to follow in Havana's El Patronato. Matilde might have felt flattered to discover that day that Harold had been shaving five years off his age, claiming he was thirty-five so as not to scare his young bride unduly. But this bride wanted a husband who was a kinder, gentler father figure than she'd had in her own father.

Their second wedding took place months later in New York City in the chapel of the Spanish-Portuguese on Central Park West. It stormed the night of that ceremony, the same night my parents set out for their honeymoon. Harold was at the wheel of the yellow Chrysler. "Lightning-proof," he said of the car to reassure her in the storm. "It's the rubber tires."

They drove up Route 17 to the Catskills, the rain a silky waterfall. Matilde removed her slip to wipe condensation from the inside of the windshield. Since there hadn't been a reception, they stopped at a diner where Matilde ordered chicken croquettes and Harold had a cheeseburger. "We got married a few hours ago!" she announced to the waitress, who put their meal on the house.

They were on their way to Grossinger's, the all-inclusive Borscht Belt resort, an odd honeymoon destination for this couple. Too much grease-laden Jewish Eastern European food was sure to stir up Matilde's gallbladder, and Harold was a man who had never associated with the sons of labor union members, men brought up hearing the Bundist politics their fathers broadcast over megaphones. Harold was an aloof Ivy Leaguer who thought nothing of attending his beloved Eli Yale football games when they fell on the High Holidays, or celebrating Christmas with his family around their small silvery-tinsel tree decorated with cobalt blue and red ornaments.

"Your grandparents telephoned every day of our honeymoon," said my mother, "and on each call, Grandma said she couldn't stand *grubeyuns*," Yiddish for vulgarians. That was who my grandmother, a rabbi's daughter, imagined populated those all-you-can-eat kosher hotels. The rabbi's daughter thought of herself as a modern woman who, as soon as she had a kitchen of her own, made pork roasts.

Matilde thought Harold looked sophisticated in his paisley smoking jacket, polishing his decanter to gleaming before he poured himself a scotch in their room. But when he offered his bride a drink, she panicked. "I told you, I never drink," she said.

Just a sip, he encouraged.

She brought the decanter to her lips. The liquid burned going down her throat and she spat out the rest like poison. Was she afraid then that her new husband would drink to the edge of cruelty like her father?

There was a time when Matilde's father, my grandfather, lived like a pasha among veiled women and bearded rabbis. He was born in 1903 in Ankara, Turkey, into a wealthy family. Like many of the stories from my maternal side of the family, his was ultimately one of loss and bad luck.

His father and uncle were rabbis. He liked to recall how his nanny and the family's cook and the maid covered their faces according to Muslim tradition. But in the presence of ten-year-old Abrahan, they smiled unchecked, unveiled. "My nanny never kissed me through her veil," Abrahan liked to say. "I was the only male that kissed her face."

After he officially became a man at his bar mitzvah in 1916, all interactions with unveiled women ended. Befitting an observant and rich family, his bar mitzvah was steeped in ritual and lavish in food. He told me he could still taste the *tishpeeshti*, a sweet Turkish cake drenched in honey. A few years later, his family dispersed—some went east to Palestine; he and the others sailed west to Cuba, where relatives had already settled. Anywhere but Turkey. Anywhere away from a place where Abrahan, as a boy on his way to school, witnessed a Turkish soldier decapitating a young Armenian man. Abuelo told me he hid in the bushes, but could not turn away. He stifled the urge to vomit. He watched with the innocent horror of a child and the innate foreboding of a Jew. When my grandfather wrapped himself in a tallit, a prayer shawl, and wound the leather straps of his tefillin, prayer boxes, around his left arm, and placed the other box on his forehead, he seemed to mourn that young man yet again. I once taped him on a reel-to-reel recorder praying in mournful, Near-Eastern singsong.

I knew those prayers, too, but when I sang along with him he stopped and told me what I was doing was *fea*, ugly, because I was a girl. *Kol isha,* the voice of a woman, was thought to be as horribly tempting as the Sirens of Greek mythology.

After Abuelo told me the story about the Armenian boy, I turned it into an English assignment in which we were to write about our families. My friend Mary's essay related that her Armenian parents were always searching for witnesses to their people's genocide. She turned away from me as I read about Abuelo's rich Turkish family. Something very bad had happened to Mary's people, and in her mind my people were the perpetrators.

"Tell her we are Jews," Abuelo said, outraged. "Tell her that we left Turkia because we were sure that we were next to be killed."

With Mary wanting to find witnesses to the Armenian genocide, I convinced her that Abuelo could help. After all, the ultimate violence is not having one's suffering acknowledged. "Who today remembers the massacre of the Armenian people?" Adolf Hitler asked in 1939. The question is emblazoned on the walls of the United States Holocaust Memorial Museum in Washington, DC.

Mary chose not to interview Abuelo. I suppose his Turkishness was too much for her, but it was just as well; I was afraid Abuelo might berate her for digging around in the painful history he claimed for himself. Whenever I asked him questions about his life he shouted that I was *muy curiosa*, and my father's warning about curiosity and the cat echoed in my mind. Unlike my father, Abuelo made me feel that my inquisitiveness was more than inappropriate; it was dangerous. I liked to think that, more than anything else, my growing detective skills at least amused my father.

Abuelo was the last older Sephardic bachelor in Havana when he met my grandmother, who was the spinsterish age of twenty-eight to his thirty-two. The story goes that he forced a kiss on her in an elevator before their date had officially started.

In their wedding picture she is plump and miserable, while he stares glassy-eyed into the camera, holding a pair of gloves. No one smiles. No one ever smiled in my mother's family. A year and a week after her wedding, Abuela gave birth to my mother.

Several weeks after my parents' honeymoon at Grossinger's, on a shopping excursion with her new mother-in-law to the Edward Malley Company, New Haven's premier department store, Matilde promptly threw up her egg salad sandwich after they stopped for lunch. "My poor boy," muttered Grandma Bolton, not for the last time.

Nine months later I was born.

CHAPTER 3

Between Home and Asylum?

At the intersection of Asylum and Farmington Avenues in Hartford, Connecticut, stands a bronze statue of Alice Cogswell, a little girl who lost her hearing at age two after a bout of meningitis rendered her, in the unfortunate parlance of the day, deaf and dumb—unable to hear or speak. The statue shows Alice standing in the palms of two enormous hands, perfectly manicured like my father's, that together form the word "light" in sign language.

Alice gave Asylum Avenue its name tangentially by virtue of the educational institution that her father, Mason Fitch Cogswell, helped establish to educate her: The Connecticut Asylum at Hartford for the Instruction of Deaf and Dumb Persons, the first of its kind in the United States. It opened its doors in 1817 and stayed in its original location on the Connecticut Turnpike/Asylum Avenue until 1921. The Asylum later changed its name to The American School for the Deaf and moved to West Hartford. By the time my family moved onto Asylum Avenue when I was three years old, the building where Alice had received her education was a mammoth insurance company.

I grew up three miles west of Alice's statue, at 1735 Asylum Avenue, on that street whose name had connotations of refuge and madness. In those matters, the address did not disappoint.

Alice was a lucky girl. Her next-door neighbor was Thomas Hopkins Gallaudet, an educator who went on to cofound and preside over the

The Bolton home at 1735 Asylum Avenue in West Hartford, Connecticut.

asylum-school. He was the first to recognize that Alice was bright, if lonely; he taught her to spell by using a stick to write in the dirt.

Her father cared enough to build Alice a school. Her neighbor cared enough to run it. Her condition insured that she would never have to hear her parents fight—as mine did, constantly, in the boxy, two-story, three-bedroom, two-and-a-half bath colonial in suburban central Connecticut that had been my mother's dream.

The house at 1735 Asylum Avenue buzzed with the potential for prosperity: It had a built-in china closet and a finished basement. It came with an electric stove.

Matilde felt she deserved this. She insisted that her lineage dated all the way back to medieval Spain: "I am a descendant of the Duke of Albuquerque, which makes me a Sephardic duchess!" I imagined her sitting on a bejeweled throne like a Disney queen, so it must have been a shock to her when the cracks in her domestic American fantasy appeared so early.

My father could barely afford the house, let alone any kind of renovation. When we moved into 1735 it was gray and beige from top to bottom;

for years we lived with the worn carpeting and peeling wallpaper of the previous occupants. My mother dreamed of decorating the house in green, her favorite color, but the painted walls and cabinets of the tiny square kitchen were thick with old brush strokes, along with raised globules of bright rubbery yellow that I could peel with my thumbnail. The inside of the cabinets, likewise densely painted, were a stop-sign red.

The finished basement flooded when it rained, shorting out the clothes dryer. The roof leaked, leaving the house vulnerable to the weather my father so carefully tracked. Still, we had the most coveted possession of any household of the era: a built-in vacuum cleaner. My mother clung to it, or to the idea of it—an all-American symbol that sparkled like the diamond ring on her left hand, the only fancy jewelry she owned. The contraption had a set of intricate tubing that connected to a growling motor and canister in the basement and on up to the top of the second floor. The thick ribbed hoses, purpose-built to fit into the wall outlets, were intimidating. But for my mother, the entire enterprise represented a sleek, modern, technologic, quintessentially American lifestyle.

There was no one to use the built-in vacuum cleaner except my mother, who cleaned on most Sundays wearing a threadbare pink-and-white bathrobe. The house shook and I trembled when she screamed her perennial refrain, also a threat: *Yo soy la criada!* I am the maid. She scrubbed the same bathroom floor over and over and broadcast that this was to be her fate—a woman who cleaned a home she did not actually own.

My mother's name was not on the deed. My father heeded his parents' legal, financial, and marital advice; they worried that my mother would walk away with all his assets should they divorce. It was a constant source of friction between my parents—whose house it was, what rights my mother had should something happen to him? What irked her more than the insolvency toward which she was certain we were headed was the gold plaque nailed to 1735 Asylum's white door, so declarative and persistent in its view that this house belonged to K. Harold Bolton, and him alone. Like his parents, my father saw the house as his most important worldly possession, and he was determined not to share it with a woman who, to him, was as volatile as the governments of the Latin American countries he had visited before he married her. Perhaps it was the only way he could control his wild and furious wife.

The house at 1735 Asylum Avenue would turn out to be the only property my father ever owned. My mother did not own the house, and never fully realized her dream of replacing the appliances or fully applying a color scheme of her own. My father was not exactly cheap and not actually poor—just a man who married at forty with no savings and no particular plan for the future. My mother's disappointment over their finances frequently curdled into rage. She threw the profusion of cash-rich Cubans of her imagination in his face: people who were able to pay their bills with money to spare. "You were born here and these refugees are doing better than us!" she yelled. "*Me limpia mi culo* with your Yale degree."

The reality was that the Cubans we knew, many of them blood relatives, mostly lived on the first floor of two-family houses that they didn't own either.

"You're bleeding us dry!" my father countered, referencing my mother's shopping expeditions downtown, where she soothed herself with purchases she carried in crisp, navy blue G. Fox & Co. bags. As evidence, he took out a piece of cardboard on which he had listed the stores to which we owed money, the sums written in blood-red ink.

"Everything I buy is on sale," my mother said. This was true; the first markdown was never enough for her. She stalked the items she wanted until the prices came down to her satisfaction.

To give herself pocket change, and perhaps rub it in that my father's income was not enough, my mother began giving impromptu Spanish lessons to neighborhood kids. The ones who didn't pass Spanish during the school year, including our paperboy, Tommy, were sentenced to summer mornings in our basement, conjugating irregular verbs in mumbled defeat. I listened to their out-of-tune recitation from the top of the basement stairs—"*Ay por Dios,*" she'd yell at her pupils, but she undercut all competitors. Hers was a cash-only business, and she saved that cash in a shoebox.

By now my sister, Carol, and the baby, John, had joined me in a house crowded with kids and chaos. The colonial at 1735 Asylum didn't have enough bedrooms for a family of five. The built-in vacuum cleaner's thick, segmented hose kinked up until there was barely any suction. Whenever the tension escalated, my mother jumped on the Asylum Avenue bus to empty my father's coffers at Lord & Taylor, or my father took off for a beer at Dino's Pizzeria. The house always felt on high alert. My mother was forever tilting toward hysteria, and my father sometimes felt it necessary to slap her out of it. "*Animál*, that's how you treat a woman?" screamed Matilde, sobbing and taking in big gulps of air as she caressed her smarting cheek. Harold the lieutenant commander saluted her and called her Sergeant Bitch.

Other times, though, he was desperate to placate her. He made a show of punishing us kids for irritating her by turning us into little soldiers and marching us around the house. During another Sunday full of dread, Aunt Reina saw us lined up in the dining room facing the wall, and cried, "It's like they're standing against Fidel's *paredón*," firing squad, she cried. I could feel the scratchy grassy wallpaper against my forehead. I felt my breath recirculating in the small space between my eyes and chin. Another time John broke away and went AWOL, toddling out to the street, where he sat defiantly cross-legged in the median of Asylum Avenue, at the intersection of crazy and refugee. The police had to halt the cars in both directions until they got my little brother back inside. When one of the cops scolded my mother for not controlling her children, she burst into raucous tears. "*Majadero!* He's a naughty little boy!"

Another policeman had to tuck me in after a domestic call to our address. I asked the officer to listen to me say the Sh'ma, my nightly prayer. "It's in Hebrew," I said. "Is that okay?" And for the moment it was. With his hat pressed against his chest, he listened intently as I affirmed God's singularity. "The Lord is one," I concluded.

As the eldest, as the one who best grasped the meaning of fights over money or about my father's romances in the years leading up to marrying so late in life, I played referee in the yellow glare of a shadeless lamp. "*No mas,*" I cried in their bedroom, and my plea would momentarily startle my parents. Sometimes I climbed onto my mother's lap and whispered, "No more crying."

When she wasn't crying, she was complaining. I overheard the confidences she whispered into the phone to her sister, my aunt Reina. "*No tenemos dinero. No puedo guantar.*" There was no money. She could not hang on. What did it mean for my mother not to be able to hang on? I pictured myself losing my grip on the monkey bars. I pictured my mother going off in a taxi to leave forever. "*Mis nervios,*" my nerves, she said, groaning and fanning herself.

Would he leave? Would she? Would they both leave me on my own to watch my younger siblings in the shambles of our house?

My father's old romances, real and imagined, were not the only spectral topics creeping into their fights. "*Ay,* I should have married Manuel," Matilde screamed at my father, who was usually silent in the face of her unrequited love for the Cuban doctor, his fury on a slow simmer, except for the time he yelled back, "Then why didn't you marry the bastard?"

Failing to get her husband properly in line, my mother turned on the three of us as we cowered in the shadows. "I should have had abortions with each of you," she announced, and now it was my turn to wail. What if, like her, I couldn't hang on? How would I manage now that my mother had wished me unborn, had sent her curse out into the universe? To hear her tell it, motherhood was the worst thing that had ever happened to her, worse even than marrying a man who disappointed her. "I could have gone to Spain to study literature at the University of Salamanca," she fretted, baiting my father to grab her by the throat and thus enable her to claim martyrdom. "I should have learned to drive a car so I could run away forever. I should have stayed in Cuba and become the biggest *comunista* in the world!"

"If you were in Cuba, you'd damn well starve in that swamp of an island," my father shouted, balling his hands into tight fists.

If there was a chance for joy in the household, it was usually with one parent or the other, never both. On Wednesdays when my father taught

The Bolton family (*left to right*): Carol, Matilde, John, Judy, and Harold, circa 1966.

night school or on a dark winter Saturday afternoon during tax season when he was out seeing clients, my mother drew the shades, as if we had to become crypto-Cubans, and we came together beneath the watchful eye of my father's naval portrait to dance and sing. My mother gathered us, her hand sitting for a moment on each of our heads as if blessing us. There was one Saturday where we started out mournfully with "Guanta-namera," softly chanting the words as if it were the Kol Nidre prayer. *Yo soy un hombre sincero,* a sincere man—a man like my father. We moved on from that sorrowful state and danced joyfully to Beny Moré's "Soy Campesino." We were those *campesinos* in the song, the same country folk that climbed Beny's *montaña querida*, his beloved mountain where he waited for his *guajira*, his gypsy.

And then my three-year-old brother, John, dancing like a wild Cubano child, the kind of child my father hadn't wanted any of us to turn into, smashed his arm straight through the window.

"*El niño esta muriendo!*" cried my mother.

"My little brother can't stop bleeding! My mommy says he's dying!" I told the operator when it was up to me to make the emergency call.

John did not die, but the gash was close to an artery and he spurted blood like a geyser. It left a stain in the second-hand carpet that lasted for years until the carpet was replaced.

Somehow, amid the chaos, my mother managed to tie a tourniquet on his arm. For all her lunacy, she could be quite resourceful. I found her scary yet irresistible throughout my childhood—I was her assistant, her sounding board, reveling in her stories of Cuba, where nothing bad ever happened. "I miss the light, the ocean breezes," my mother always said.

"Don't marry a *viejo*," she warned me. "An old man has too many tras-tiendas, and those secrets will make everyone tired."

She was certain that my father had mistresses aplenty; any time there was a wrong number or a hang-up she was sure it was one of his lovers. "Your father is so old he must have had another wife before me," she said, the opening salvo to her stories of children he must have fathered in the distant past. "One day a girl will walk up to you and say she is your sister. Don't let her take your money." I was nine years old and didn't have any money, so I didn't see the danger of this happening, but the older I got and the more my mother repeated and embellished her stories—adding, subtracting, shaping the ongoing narrative that streamed from beneath my parents' bedroom door—the more the stories that once fascinated me became tired litanies.

By the time I was eleven, I was done with her tales. "It's boring," I said as she once again told me her favorite story of a little girl who became separated from her mother in a busy marketplace in Turkey, a dangerous place where my grandfather was born and where genies hid in lamps and soldiers rounded up Armenians with an eye toward killing the Jews, too.

"A policeman found a little girl just like you crying for her mother," she whispered in my darkened bedroom. "When he asked her what her mother looked like, the girl said she was the most beautiful woman in her village. And so the prettiest women in the village were gathered together like they were in a beauty contest, but none of them was the little girl's mother. Suddenly the girl ran toward a very *fea* wrinkled woman without teeth and hugged her. 'This is my mother,' she said, as if she had won the greatest prize in the whole wide world."

I intuited that this was my mother's way of instilling loyalty. She needed me to understand that she was the only one, the only mother in the world, no matter what, no matter when, no matter if she aged.

During her stormiest moods my father—always respectful of changes in the weather—couldn't withstand the gale force. We went with him to seek refuge at the duck pond on the grounds of The American School for the Deaf. "Stay close," my father said as the three of us followed him around the pond. My mother's curse—"Go, drown with the ducks"—rang in our ears. We trooped by another statue of Alice, a replica of one on the campus of Gallaudet University in Washington, DC, in which she leans against her teacher as he teaches her to spell the letter *A* for Alice. We assembled behind Dad to feed the ducks chunks of stale poppy seed rolls, like an improvised ceremony of the *tashlich* ritual.

The Hebrew word *tashlich* literally means to cast off, and refers to the symbolic and communal ceremony performed on the second day of Rosh Hashana. The point is to purge the previous year's sins, represented in the pieces of bread thrown into a body of water. Verses from the prophet Micah, recited during tashlich, portray a forgiving, loving God ready to receive our apologies. "You do not maintain anger forever but You delight in loving-kindness. You will again have compassion upon us, subduing our sins, casting all our sins into the depths of the sea."

I threw chunks of poppy seed roll into the water and recited the litany of my sins in the hope that God would forgive me:

For the sin of laughing

For the sin of setting the table the wrong way

For the sin of flushing my vitamins down the toilet

For the sin of having common brown eyes

For the sin of being born.

CHAPTER 4

English Only

"*raidor*," traitor! That's what my mother called my father for having had a life before he met her, but the only traitor I knew of was Benedict Arnold, and my father wasn't a bit like that. He wasn't a white-wigged turncoat—he was a patriot who revered the flag, which he waved on every national holiday.

In the days when he was still energetic, still in command, one of the most American things my all-American father did was to orchestrate the summer cookouts. He happily grilled hamburgers as he wore red, white, and blue plaid shorts. Orange-over-blue charcoal flames licked patties of meat as he hummed the John Philip Sousa marches blasting from the speakers he set up at my little brother's bedroom window.

The world shook with my father's fervent patriotism. It was an earthquake that combined his love of music with his love for "the greatest country on earth."

"There's nothing more American than John Philip Sousa's music," he said. "You three over here," he ordered, arranging us. "Here you go, each of you have your own flag." We traipsed around the yard to the loud brassy beat.

No matter how long my Cuban relatives had been in the United States, my father's patriotism both frightened and baffled them. When they came to Asylum Avenue for sunny summer cookouts in the backyard that my father proudly measured at an acre, Aunt Reina, Tio José,

and my abuelos brought offerings of tostones and corn tamales, but kept
their distance from him.

I was a child of both worlds and belonged to neither. But occasionally
both of those worlds came together. With the marching music pounding
from John's window, I left the dull confines of my Connecticut backyard
and pretended I was in Havana. "Today is as hot as Cuba," I announced to
my relatives with confidence.

"But there were ocean breezes, *niña*," my mother countered. My relatives agreed that a walk along the sea wall on the Malecón was the cool-
est on a warm day. I marched to Sousa around the backyard's perimeter:
"*Mira, estoy caminando en el Malecón!*"

"*Que es esta locura?*" What is this craziness, my abuelo asked of the
trilling piccolos threading through the declarative "Stars and Stripes Forever." "It sounds like whistling."

I always had the feeling that with these commemorative displays, my
father was staring down his memories of the war, in which he was back
on his supply ship issuing orders to men nearly twice his age. He was
proud of what he had done during the four years he served his country in
the South Pacific.

In stark contrast, my mother's version of Cuba was a cautionary tale.
I was a bilingual baby born on December 30, 1960, five days before Washington and Havana severed diplomatic ties on January 3, 1961. Three
months later, when Cuban exiles united as Brigade 2506 to overthrow
Castro at the Bay of Pigs, my grandmother—my abuela, who had come to
the United States to help care for me—insisted on rejoining her family in
Havana. She was particularly worried about her son, who at nineteen
was ripe for Castro's revolutionary army.

Much has been made in family lore of Abuela taking off on one of the
last direct flights from the United States to Cuba. She found her way back
to Connecticut a year later with Abuelo and my aunt Reina's family. But
on that April day in 1961, stout and determined, Abuela made my father
promise he would find a way to bring my uncle José over as soon as possible. José was still young enough to qualify for the rescue operation
called Pedro Pan, which between 1960 and 1962 ferried fourteen thou-

sand children away from a Cuba that might eventually have conscripted them into the army. Some of them went to live with relatives; others went into foster care across thirty states.

My father kept his word. José arrived in Miami in June 1961, even though the Cuban authorities tried to ground his plane full of Pedro Pan kids as it readied for takeoff at José Martí Airport. My uncle, of the thick Buddy Holly glasses, oily pompadour, and prominent Adam's apple, waited for a connecting flight to Hartford. All around him were the sounds of a language that reminded him of the squawking of farm animals. The disorientation of not being able to read signs or understand announcements competed with his nervousness about living in a new country with a much older brother-in-law he had never met.

Dad was forty-two to José's nineteen, more like father and son, though perhaps without the warmth. My father adored practicing his Spanish, albeit plodding through the language at gringo speed, yet he insisted that my uncle immediately leap into the bubbling cauldron of American assimilation. This made us a motley crew—my father, my mother, Uncle José, and me, still in the crib. My father was determined to stamp out any lingering trace of Cuba in my uncle, insisting that José learn English right away and imparting daily lessons on pronunciation and usage.

José's first job in the United States was to pluck feathers from freshly slaughtered chickens. "This is how you start off in America," said Dad, "from the bottom."

José lasted a day. By the end of the week he was pressing clothes at a dry cleaner's while taking English lessons at night. Then it was on to bookkeeping and other odd jobs. He waited at bus stops in the January cold, more than determined to become the man my father insisted he be.

The first English he must have learned was "English only!" That was the phrase my father kept bellowing. José was Dad's American project, an endeavor to which he wholeheartedly dedicated himself. To that end, he declared the bilingual apartment in East Hartford an English-only zone. He forbade even my mother from speaking her native tongue lest it impede José's assimilation. He drilled my teenage uncle in vocabulary and American idioms: Has the cat got your tongue? A coward dies a thousand deaths.

Meanwhile, Matilde and José continued to speak Spanish to each other while listening for my father's quick and deliberate footfalls on the stairs to the second-floor East Hartford apartment. Mostly they spoke in whispers, afraid to be caught in a loop of Spanish. They were like crypto-Jews during the Inquisition who prayed in Hebrew under cover of deepest night.

"Damn it, he'll never be fluent if you keep spoiling him," my father yelled when he caught them. "English only!"

"Harold, he's exhausted from trying to think in English all day," my mother said. "I know how he feels."

My mother had been honing her English by watching soap operas like *As the World Turns* and *Guiding Light*. She considered the characters her friends for years after she stopped watching.

"I sorry," said José.

"I AM sorry," corrected my father. "I am, you are, he is."

As my parents' first-born, I was the only one of their three children to speak Spanish fluently, and I intuited early on that everything was better for my mother in Spanish. With Spanish she retreated into another world, one in which the harsh Teutonic name Matilda was softened with an *e* at the end.

She was calmer in Spanish. More articulate. She was not as prone to fake a suicide attempt, my father's razor hovering over the ropy veins of her wrist. On the nights my father, staunch and formal, left the house for three glorious hours to teach accounting at the University of Hartford, we were festive—speaking Spanish, eating TV dinners on trays in the den, even breaking Dad's "no singing at the table" rule with a songfest. "*Mis hijos,*" my children, my mother said expansively. She would give us an impromptu Spanish lesson, pointing to her nose (*el nariz*), her mouth (*la boca*), her teeth (*los dientes*). "My children have large foreheads because they are brilliant," she trilled in Spanish.

On nights like those I stayed up past my bedtime, watching *What in the World?*, a travel show taped in one of Channel 3's flimsy studios on

Constitution Plaza. We pretended that we, too, had been to classic landmarks like the Taj Mahal and the Eiffel Tower, even though it was only my father who had traveled anywhere. He had been to such far-flung places as Australia and the Philippines and Guatemala. My mother had never changed time zones.

With Dad out of the house, we turned up the hi-fi to spin ourselves into star-flecked dizziness. My mother danced with us and then broke away so that I orbited her as if she were a golden sun of sharp, hot rays. When she danced alone, she did so with one hand on her stomach, the other raised in the air as if taking an oath. "*Hay Cuba, como te extraño,*" how she longed for Cuba. It was in the swing of her hips, the sweetness of her song. She danced as if she were the only Cubana left in the world.

My father inherited his patriotic DNA from his father before him. America was everything to Grandpa Bolton, who had changed the family name from Bolotin to ensure that his children assimilated even further into the American fabric. This was a country that had enabled him, an immigrant from Ukraine, to receive a high-profile education at Yale and later to send his only son to the same institution. Although the birth of my aunt Gladys in 1914 exempted Grandpa from conscription in World War I, his son responded to the call that his country needed him. My father enlisted in the Navy on the cusp of World War II, just before he graduated from Yale.

Dad lived his entire life in the land of the free and the home of the brave, but he also wanted to distinguish himself from his father by taking up a grand, personal adventure. He served on a naval supply ship in World War II, drifting and dreaming and ultimately steaming ahead in the Pacific to the Philippines, to magical places that his father could only imagine. Tiny fragments of my father's escapades gleamed in the light of story. "In Sydney, I broke up a barroom brawl between my men and a posse of Australian sailors," he told us. He let slip that he'd been in an Australian military hospital for two months. "A fungal infection. Picked it up in the Philippines."

William M. Bolton's 1913 graduation from the
Sheffield Scientific School of Yale College.

Dad and Grandpa and Grandma Bolton were of their time. My father was born at the beginning of 1919 in New Haven, on the second floor of a two-family house my grandparents owned on Ellsworth Avenue. Woodrow Wilson, the stony-faced Princetonian, was president at the time, negotiating placebo treaties in top hat and tails. Modernity and Puritanism mingled as child labor laws, pure-food laws, free verse, and Prohibition were all in play. The gross national product tripled and the national debt went from one billion to twenty-four billion dollars. A jury acquitted eight baseball players from the Chicago White Sox of throwing the World Series to the Cincinnati Reds, but barred them for life from the game.

Mobility was on the rise—faster cars, changing neighborhoods, increased consumption. Toys, stocks, and birth control were for sale; my grandparents bought all three. Energy was abundant and houses were wired for electricity. Cars reached grand speeds of forty miles per hour. Life was moving fast, and my grandparents were early adopters of the changes that went with it.

By 1919 World War I was over, but the Bolshevik Revolution was in full swing; my father, the fervent anti-Communist, lived since birth with Russia menacing him. City dwellers boarded trains that brought them to the shore. Swimming in the ocean became a national pastime. My grandparents rented a summer beach house in Old Saybrook, Connecticut—a town name that sounded fresh and breezy. It was a place that accepted the Boltons over the Hurwitzes, relatives who tried to rent there, too. My grandfather had the chutzpah to pass, the nerve to hobnob with the sons of Connecticut Yankees.

My grandfather did well in the stock market. He drank illegal liquor to keep warm at his alma mater's football games. Walter Camp, the father of American football and the coach of the Yale team, introduced calisthenics and packaged them for America as part of the daily dozen. Hemlines rose, although my grandmother still could not vote.

The tango was forbidden. Ragtime was "Black music," yet too good to be ignored. A Jew named Irving Berlin wrote "Alexander's Ragtime Band"; thirty years later he sealed his fame with a song called "White Christmas." My grandfather established an orchestra with a Yale classmate,

Jack Cipriano, and the Bolton-Cipriano Orchestra specialized in Viennese light opera and Gilbert and Sullivan, which they played up and down the East Coast at exclusive fraternities and debutante balls.

Dad could lose himself in the Viennese waltzes that Grandpa played so passionately on his violin. From vestiges of his travels in Latin America, he crossed over to love the dream-laden music of Spain. The clashing percussion of bullfighting music and the rousing *zarzuelas* brought out a life force in him he otherwise rarely showed the world.

He took his love of Spanish music to the airwaves for two hours on Sunday afternoons to broadcast a show he called *The Music of Spain*. My father had somehow collected hundreds of imported records with covers showing bullfights and ladies dressed in mantillas. All of this happened from the Hartford studios of WEXT, a country and western music station that donated space and time for community programming during the otherwise dull, blue-law Sunday.

On the air, my father frequently touted the fact that there were twenty Spanish-speaking countries right in the US's backyard. For him, that alone upgraded Spanish and the countries that spoke it. After all, he had traded in his college French for Spanish. Yet he couldn't separate his love of language from his political analyses. At my parents' parties, with a few drinks in him, he noted that Latin America with its shaky governments was paternalistic. His complicated relationship with Latin America weirdly jibed with the troubling events in his marriage. In the often tense times in their relationship, he said my mother was as unbalanced as the governments of the continent to our south. But, in the end, Spanish was romantic for him. The most romantic of the romance languages, he told my mother. It was the kind of comment that passed for love between them.

In a black-and-white picture of my father playing weekend deejay, scattered white lines break up the photograph's gloss. K. Harold Bolton wears a no-nonsense white shirt, black pants, and a five-o'clock shadow, even though the clock in the picture is just coming up on twelve-fifteen p.m. In his left hand is a stopwatch. Behind him are consoles with large buttons and instruments to gauge sound levels—instruments that look

Harold Bolton hosting his weekly Sunday radio show,
The Music of Spain, on WEXT.

as if they belonged in a war room rather than a radio station. In front are
two turntables unfurling *paso doble* music. I know this from the record
cover propped up nearby, announcing in a ribbony script: *Suspiros de
España*, Spanish marching music that has an accompanying paso doble,
a two-step dance that acts out the drama of the bullfight. Traditionally,
the man is the matador and the woman his cape, which he whips around.
The woman can also take on the role of the bull or an adoring señorita
dancing flamenco by herself, much the way my mother did her own pri-

vate two-step. My father is offering a toothy grin that announces a happiness born of music and memory.

"*Caballeros y damas,*" he says into a large microphone suspended from the ceiling. Gentlemen and Ladies. His voice pours out of the radio and fills the house, his heavy American Spanish so distinct from my mother's light, high-pitched version. We gather around the radio with my mother and thrill to the sound of his voice. In that moment, my father is a celebrity. Despite his accent, he has known all things Spanish for a very long time.

And yet, English only. My uncle José heard those words as he loaded the dry-cleaning machine with solvent. He heard them on the lonely, dimly lit bus ride home from night classes. He heard and he obeyed until he shakily began to string sentences together, until he thought in English, until he recited the Pledge of Allegiance without prompting.

Until he raised his right hand a decade later and became a US citizen.

CHAPTER 5

The Summer of Ana

The summer of Ana began with a knock at the door in 1972.

Ana was a teenage exchange student from Guatemala who was staying with a local family. Somehow, she had made her way to us through the town's small Latino circuit, although it was curious that of all the places where Ana could have landed in the United States, she ended up in West Hartford.

Ana's skin was the color of café con leche, her eyes blacker than the olives we ate out of the can. She dazzled me. Her goal that summer was to "espeake Engleesh good," and what better way than to practice the language with three children of a man who had been to Guatemala? A man who had loved it there, who had posed for a picture in Lake Atitlan in 1952, the very year Ana was born.

That summer, Ana spent entire weekends with us, and I could hear my parents fighting at night: "You are in love with that *india*," my mother shouted.

My father absorbed the accusation. His rigid silence infuriated my mother; she made dark hints about Ana's origins.

"She's with us too much. And she's a *chusma*. Look at her feet!" Ana had made the mistake of wearing sandals that showed off her polished toenails, something nearly as vulgar to my mother as walking around topless.

My mother often called me india too. In the makeshift caste system of Latin America, an india was an untouchable who went unnoticed as she cleaned or served in a *gallego* home. I was an india when I disobeyed one of my mother's draconian laws about dressing or comportment: An india like me wears any old *trapo* outside the house. An india like me never brushes her hair so that she has a headful of *bolones*, knots.

When Ana was with us, life was expansive, full of youthful possibility. The booth at Howard Johnson's on Sunday night went from barely fitting the five of us to accommodating six splendidly. At the All You Can Eat Spaghetti Night, my father suspended his moratorium on sugary drinks: "You can have root beers tonight!" He was as relaxed as I'd seen him.

"*Un placer*," a pleasure, he whispered just loud enough for me to hear.

"*Que rico!*" Ana exclaimed, clapping her hands.

My father passed the glasses around. "Drink up," he encouraged while my mother fumed.

"*No estan acomstubrados*," my mother said, trying to take the drinks away from us, spilling soda. "Look what you made me do," she said to no one in particular as the tears came. "Harold, they'll get sick," she persisted.

But Ana prevailed. We all saw how my father went quieter, became softer with her around. "You stare too much at her," my mother accused him.

"Don't be ridiculous; you project too damn much," he said, coming out of the sweet trance in which Ana had put him.

I loved Ana all the more for bringing about this transformation. Ana was a party. A celebration. That summer, she mingled at my parents' Saturday night fiestas, the dining room table laden with South American potluck and syrupy flans. The party regulars included Uruguayan friends of my parents, who brought *empanadas, tortas fritas*, and *bizcochos*—gigantic cookies coated with sugar. A poet from Spain with three names that sounded disconsonant together was another regular at these parties, and at the ready to recite his verses of love. The only other person I knew who had three names was my father's musical hero, the March King, John Philip Sousa. My father led the trio of gringos that night, including Jack Laflin and his wife, Vivian. Jack spoke a gringo-inflected Spanglish of his own creation, just a notch below my father's proficiency in Spanish. He got a kick out of calling my father Haroldo.

My father loved the pulp-fiction novels that Jack published in the 1960s. As far as I could tell, writing those books was the only job Jack had. The slim paperbacks were overwrought spy novels full of hackneyed glamor and prose as purple as a bruise. A cigar in one hand, a strong gin and tonic in the other, Jack sloppily told the poet, "I barely understand a word of the lovelorn *basura* you write." The poet, enraged, turned on his heels and marched to the other side of the living room.

Then it was that time in the party when my father woke my little sister and scooped her up in his arms. He took her downstairs and waltzed her across the room. He did not notice that I was following them. He drunkenly declared Ana and my sister looked so much alike that "they could be sisters!"

Jack patted my father on the back. "You old son of a gun, Haroldo," he laughed.

"Stop talking *boberias*," nonsense, my mother said, almost tripping in her haste to grab Carol away.

Back upstairs, I eventually fell asleep to the vibration of conversations, laughter, and the music from the records from Spain and Latin America that my father collected. He stacked them on the Magnavox hi-fi's automatic record changer, and the music flowed with the liquor. At the end of those nights, my mother sang "Guantanamera." The poet played the guitar. When I listened to her, I thought, this is what crying sounds like in song.

I was eleven to Ana's twenty, and keenly aware of numbers. They had a magic about them, sometimes an evil magic. When we were on the road in our '65 Chevy Malibu, I added up the numbers I saw on license plates. In Hebrew school, I noted the bundles of sevens and tens and forties through which Jewish history unfolded. "I'll be dead by the time I'm forty," my mother told us too often, because she was *inervada*—her nerves were about to strangle her to death.

My mother was scared of growing old. Bound up in that lifelong sorrow was the loss of her youthful self, the girl who had nearly been the belle of the ball. She inflated the honor of being runner-up in the Queen Esther pageant of 1954 into a victory all its own. "Look at those girls," she said any time she saw a beauty pageant on television. "I was prettier than any of them."

She had a point. The proof is in a black-and-white photograph taken of her at nineteen, almost the same age as Ana that summer. The photo shoot had been a prize for identifying the Glenn Miller song "Chattanooga Choo Choo" on the radio. The photographer turned Matilde's head slightly to the right to look as if she were gazing into the future. Her wavy black hair is loose and cascades down her back. Her lips are dark, her eyebrows arched like a movie star's.

Nineteen-year-old Matilde Alboukrek in Havana, Cuba.

At nineteen, my mother was nobody's runner-up. She was magnificent. But she could not stop Ana, or the fear of what Ana represented, from overtaking her.

Ana often went with us on our weekly Sunday afternoon trips to Grandma and Grandpa Bolton's sweet gingerbread house on Stimson Road in New Haven—the house with the rose bushes and the birdbath in the backyard. Waxed fruit sat atop their gleaming mahogany dining room table, and the gilded, lettered spines of Reader's Digest books lined their bookshelves in the living room. Grandpa's wide, green Oldsmobile sat in his driveway like a stoic elder. Sipping chicken soup at Grandma's smooth dining room table, Ana said, "I'm wishing to bring back this *sopa* to Guatemala." Grandpa gave her roses from his garden, and she carried bunches of them in her arms like a bride. Grandma smiled and said, "My name is Anna, too."

Over and over, I heard my mother plead with my father, "Who is she? Who is she, really?"

He didn't answer. If he had been drinking, he went silent, twiddling his fingers in a crazy sign language only he understood. The most he would do is what he always did when he couldn't bear it: he fled to the Malibu and took sanctuary in the driver's seat. I heard the door slam from my room and knew my father was inside the car, breathing heavily. He barely backed out of the driveway before abruptly putting the car in drive. Back and forth, back and forth. He finally came to a dead stop with his head against the steering wheel.

Upstairs, lying in my bed with me, my mother trembled. In response to her fear over Ana and what she meant to my father, and his storming out of the house, she came down with a migraine. I brought her a cold washcloth to cover her eyes and block out the slightest pain-inducing light.

Ana also went with us on the long car rides to Westchester to visit my father's best friend, Felipe. She held Carol on her lap, quelling Carol's carsickness. As we pulled up, Felipe's wife, Maria Elena, was giving two of their young sons haircuts on the deck of the house.

"Ana, how wonderful to see you," said Felipe, extending his hand to her. He said it as if he had not seen her in years.

Judy and Ana Hernandez on Felipe's deck, circa 1971.

My father and Felipe had been friends for more than two decades. We spent many summer Sundays at Felipe's backyard parties, a passel of kids splashing in the big aluminum tub of a swimming pool. On that afternoon, my father talked too much about a past of which neither my mother nor we three children were a part. "I was a different guy back then," he said, looking at Ana, his grin wide and loud.

"*Borracho,*" my mother muttered. Old drunk.

My father clinked glasses with his longtime friend. He made sloppy, rum-laden toasts to *amor, salud, mujeres y tiempo para gosarlos.* To love, to health, to women and the time to enjoy them. One of Felipe's kids, who knew I was afraid to put my face in the water, pulled me under in the pool until my father noticed I was missing. I saw my dad in sharp focus through the transparent ceiling of water just before he rescued me.

After that summer, Ana left as suddenly as she had appeared. She caused a before-and-after shift in us and, as a family, we were never the same. Once Ana departed, my father retreated to his narrow closet to drink. He refused to offer any explanation, other than to enrage my mother periodically by describing Ana as "*muy linda y muy dulce*," beautiful and sweet like candy.

It was the last time I saw Ana, but I never forgot her and neither did my mother. She hated when I named my first child Anna, after my grandmother. It was the American name Grandma chose after she abandoned her Yiddish one, Chenke. With its extra *n*, it was the Anglicized spelling of Ana.

"How could you name my granddaughter after my mother-in-law who treated me like *porqueria*," crap, my mother screamed.

I knew the name thrilled my father, though, even though by then his mind had deteriorated along with his Parkinson's-addled body. Grandma had been dead for almost twenty years when her namesake was born. "Who's here?" my father asked. Then it struck me: Maybe he thought Ana was in the room with him when he heard me call the baby by her name.

"You crazy old man," my mother seethed as he held the new baby with my help. "This is Judy's baby!"

Anna, his mother's name. Anna, his grandchild.

"Ana," said my father, using the Spanish pronunciation, his voice soft and hoarse from disease. "A beautiful name for a beautiful girl." It was the last he would say on the subject for the rest of his life.

I had somehow thought my father might live until the end of time, raspy and small, forced to listen to the deafening soundtrack of cable television in his La-Z-Boy chair. Lost forever in a storm of backfiring neurotransmitters, the consequence of which was that, eventually, he no longer knew me.

At the exact moment he died in 2002 I was with my daughter, then eight, in a line to buy challah for Rosh Hashana that snaked past three storefronts. Rather than the typical braided loaf, the Rosh Hashana challah is round in shape, symbolizing the cycles of life, the majestic shape of the Earth, the never-ending generations. Anna and I bought four of these round challahs, along with two loaves of sweet flaky chocolate babka, two loaves of spongy honey cake, and an apple pie for the dinner we planned to make that weekend. Those last two desserts were meant to complement the apples we would dip in honey with the hope for a sweet new year.

We pulled up at four o'clock with a trunk full of baked goods and crumbs of sugar cookies on our lips. My husband, Ken, was waiting at the end of the driveway, hands behind his back, pacing. I knew my father had died before I even got out of the car.

As we went about planning my father's funeral, my mother concurrently planned her own. She believed that whatever we chose for Dad—a traditional shroud or regular clothing—would be her fate, too.

Mort, the aptly named undertaker, watched us volley back and forth about how best to bury my father. He clasped his hands as if prayerful on his elegant black desk, while my siblings and I pushed for the plain pine box of a traditional Jewish burial and my mother held out for the $10,000 burnished mahogany-finished number, "the Cadillac of coffins," according to Mort.

The irony was that my father had always been a Chevy kind of guy. I couldn't shake the feeling that I had cheated a humble man out of a humble funeral.

At the cemetery in Avon, a suburb trying hard to be country chic, the open grave looked too big, then too small. Rabbit hole. Hellhole. A gaping hole that the mourners had to fill with no expectation of anything in return. *Chesed shel Emet*—the truest act of kindness. Dad's best friend from college, Maish, shoveled in large clumps of dirt that thwacked against the coffin. Once, twice, three times. My friends Miriam and Ze'ev were next. When I reached out to take the shovel from Miriam, she stayed my hand and stabbed the mound of dirt with the shovel so that it stood upright; just as dying is a solitary act, each person must confront death alone. Each person must take a shovel that stands on its own.

I shoveled furiously, but did not come close to filling the hole. There was nothing more I could do for my father, nor he for me.

Part II

CHAPTER 6

Mourning Harold

The rabbis of the Talmud have a lengthy discussion about a soul that is neither living nor dead—a *goses*. They illustrate the point with a story about Rabbi Judah, whose students tried to prevent his soul from departing to heaven by praying that he live, while the angels prayed for his earthly existence to come to an end. The rabbi's maid took matters into her own hands and shouted from the rooftop, "May the prayers of mortals overwhelm the prayers of the angels!" When she witnessed Rabbi Judah's suffering, however, she changed her mind: "May the prayers of the angels overwhelm the prayers of the mortals!" Her prayer was not powerful enough to override those of the rabbi's students, so she distracted them by smashing a pitcher. Momentarily startled, the students stopped praying long enough for Rabbi Judah's soul to escape his tormented body.

I thought about that story after my father died. Somewhere, the pitcher had smashed. The prayers of the angels, along with my prayers, had prevailed.

The night before I buried my father, I lay on one of the twin beds in the pink-shag-rug, poster-plastered bedroom of my girlhood, paging through the tattered prayer book from which I had prayed in Jewish Day School. It was small and square, the kind of book I'd seen women holding at the Western Wall, the *kotel*, in Jerusalem. With its bakery-tissue-thin pages that made it seem a lesser prayer book came a false modesty that forbade women to participate fully in Jewish ritual—a false modesty that diminished a woman's place in Jewish life.

The prayer book contained line after line of tiny Hebrew letters that I could no longer read fluently. I stumbled through the Kaddish prayer—the Orphan's Kaddish, the prayer of mourning—spoken in the chewy language of Aramaic but rendered in Hebrew letters. The first time I heard the Kaddish, I was young—a single-digit age—and attending traditional Sephardic High Holiday services with my mother and her parents. When it came time for the Kaddish, almost everyone rose and I did, too. I suddenly felt Abuela's hand clamp down on my shoulder. "*Barminam,*" she hissed in Ladino, which loosely translates as God forbid. If I continued to stand, my faux pas might have broken a pitcher and shortened the lifespan of one of my relatives.

The Kaddish prayer originated around the ninth century, a date that corresponds to Rav Amram Gaon's prayer book, in which biblical archeologists found the earliest surviving text of the Kaddish. Some five hundred years before that, there is an explanation in the *Targum Yerushalmi*, a book that gathers together paraphrases, explanations, and interpretations of the Bible, that the Kaddish of today bears similarities to the Kaddish that Jacob and his sons recited.

In Jewish tradition, a child says the Kaddish for a parent every day for eleven months. Originally this was only for sons, but now daughters have full access to the prayer, too, within a minyan, or prayer quorum. The idea of confronting grief and sorting through memories for a stretch of time appealed to me and intimidated me. "You are not required to do the task," says the Talmud, "but neither are you free to desist from it."

Throughout the various strands of Judaism I had practiced in my lifetime, that Talmudic maxim hovered over my hyphenated identities—American-Jew, Cuban-American, Cuban-Jew (Jubana), Sephardic-Ashkenazic, Yiddish-Ladino-knowing Jew—but saying the Kaddish for my father, even if only for thirty days and not the full eleven months, was a daunting prospect. Nevertheless, I thought of the Kaddish as a spiritual jetpack strapped to a parent's soul, helping it to arrive in heaven. A righteous soul can make the final leg of the trip—that is the twelfth month—

on its own power. The assumption is that all parents have been righteous in their own way and can make that final push on their own.

Jewish day school was now in my distant past. I wasn't sure I had the stamina for daily prayer anymore. Was I enough of a believer to say the Kaddish, an extended valentine, to a God who had taken my father from me?

I traced my complicated connection to religion to the highly Orthodox Hebrew Academy of Greater Hartford I attended from sixth to ninth grades. I ended up there after my mother pulled me out of public school to ward off any exposure to sex education. My father had been adamantly against my leaving the public Morley School; in his eyes, going to the Hebrew Academy kicked me all the way back to a shtetl way of life.

The Hebrew Academy ran like a traditional yeshiva—literally, a place to study Torah. The summer before I entered, I slogged through hours of Hebrew lessons to get up to speed, learning the austere alphabet and sounding out the words as if there were several feet of dark space between each letter. I imagined scarily bearded teachers booming holy words that barely came into shape—teachers who looked like the sepia picture of my great-grandfather Rabbi Abraham Rosen.

Instead, my first Hebrew teacher was a lovely, modest young woman named Gloria. I sounded out the words that she taught me in her rabbi father's study as we sat crowded in among long, thick black books with gold-lettered spines: "So much learning," Gloria said dreamily.

Among the rules of the yeshiva was that, as a girl, my clothing had to be modest, covering elbows and knees. I was not allowed to wear pants, as per the stern collection of rabbis at the school. Stockings or tights had to cover the legs at all times. I sat in the cramped women's section during prayers, watching short, doughy, post-bar mitzvah boys play with the fringes of their new prayer shawls while stumbling through a cluster of Hebrew blessings thanking God for not making them heathens, slaves, or women. From the beginning, I wanted my words to move just a few feet, out of the dingy cramped section where I had to sit and into the bright sacred area I could glimpse through the small square cutout in the make-shift wall. "Segregation," my father grumbled when I told him about the synagogue configuration at the Hebrew Academy. Segregation defined me on the other side of the *mechitzah* in the women's section, and in my life.

My father had fashioned a religion for himself that was an amalgam of American patriotism and Yale history. The Yale Bowl was his sanctuary, *The Yale Football Story* his prayer book. America was his deity. In his view, our association with the yeshiva erased all the progress his family had made in assimilating to America. "These people don't even turn on a light on Saturday. They'd rather sit in the dark," he groused.

My mother, on the other hand, called upon her own Jewish day school experience from Cuba, although hers was a less stringent Judaism. After Sabbath morning services, she walked along the Malecón in Havana, *meneando*—swinging her backside just on the right side of decent for a Latina Jewish girl. "I had the most beautiful legs in Havana," she said. Deep into middle age and beyond, my mother still walked *meneando*. "I'm pretty yet," she said, even as an old woman when her top denture slipped out of place.

During my time at the yeshiva I turned twelve—which, according to exacting Jewish law, made me a daughter of the commandments in anticipation of menstruation. When I got my period later that year, I learned I was marked as ritually impure: *tumah*. It was also the year that the science teacher Mrs. Bernstein, a pious woman who covered her hair as yet another sign of modesty, had a breakdown in class. "Menstrual blood," she screamed, "is the reason women cannot say the blessings over the Torah! But it is the purest blood in the world!"

Under a harsh fluorescent reality, the boys lorded it over us girls, taunting us that we were not allowed to read from or even touch the Torah. They reveled in the blessings that thanked God for not making them like the hapless girls behind the divider. Mostly, though, the boys were bored, the girls resigned. "Do you think we'll ever lead prayers?" I asked my friend Shoshana. She pursed her lips. "I don't think so," she said sadly. "At least not here."

Rather than drawing away from all this, I became an Orthodox Jew, much to the dismay of both my parents. I kept kosher in our nonkosher kitchen, which wasn't easy for any of us. I starved myself rather than enter a kitchen full of forbidden meats mixing with all kinds of dairy. I stockpiled crackers and cans of tuna that I ate on paper plates in my room. I sucked on Italian ices to help stay kosher until I had starved myself down to eighty pounds.

Observing the Sabbath, too, was problematic at 1735 Asylum—particularly when daylight stretched later into the night hours. Those long days reminded me of the way I counted off the minutes, the hours, in school. Judaism for me at that time was about getting through rigor and formality. I did not pass the time in any sort of religious reverie. Sitting in Hebrew class was about the fear that manifested the first time I noticed the backs of my knees and my armpits drenched in the sweat of anxiety as my heart sped and my breathing became shallow. It was about a new awareness: depression. I was the thin, slight girl who arranged my food in advance of the Sabbath, since lighting a fire and using electricity to cook was expressly forbidden. I removed the light bulb from the refrigerator so as not to symbolically spark a flame by turning on a light. I rushed to tear toilet paper in advance, to avoid ripping, which was considered a prohibited form of labor on the Sabbath.

My father was silent and angry with me. My mother screamed that I was *loca* and dragged me to doctors. "Nervous like the mother," muttered one of them as he listened to my heart.

None of the grown-ups around me saw my rigid piousness for what it was—a rebellion, a need for individuality, and also a search for structure in my messy home life. My parents tried to bully me out of my Orthodoxy, effectively holding me hostage on the Sabbath, knowing I would not ride in a car. They forbade me to walk a mile to the nearest Orthodox synagogue or spend Saturdays with my religious friends. "You will never be one of those unsupervised *pilluelos*," urchins, my mother said. Or, alternatively, "I'm going to commit you to the Institute for Living if you don't stop this *locura!*"

"Go ahead," I dared her. I had read Sylvia Plath and there was something romantic about going away for a long medical rest to a psychiatric hospital. Meanwhile, I retaliated by swaying to prayer and crying myself to sleep until the sun set again.

Heathen, slave, woman.

My mother came up with a new weapon to cure me of too much Jewishness: Right after the Hebrew Academy, she sent me to the all-girls, all-Catholic Mount Saint Joseph. My father had no opinion about this decision.

I was not the first in my family to go to the nuns. Abuela had learned to crochet and speak French in a convent school in Greece. Nuns tutored my mother in literature when she was in high school at the Instituto. In America, my mother briefly taught Spanish at the Saint Agnes Home for Unwed Mothers, and then for twenty years at Northwest Catholic High School.

Sending me to the Mount seemed like a good compromise for everyone. This all-girls school proved to have the structure and strictures that I craved. It had the formality and gravitas to match my mother's memories of nuns in wimples.

The people at the yeshiva thought I had become a political prisoner: "It's not right for a Jewish girl to go to a Catholic school!"

I was also not the first Jew to attend the Mount. In the '50s and '60s, the Mount had a sterling academic reputation, and there was a cadre of girls like me who couldn't see themselves going to prep schools like Miss Porter's or Ethel Walker. By the time I arrived at the Mount in the 1970s, changing mores and attrition had taken their toll. I plopped down in a place of dull wood floors that were once waxed every day, and fraying maroon velvet curtains that indicated the school had once seen days of glory. Large crucifixes with a half-naked Jesus nailed to them—the Mount's version of erotic mezuzahs, I supposed—floated above me. It seemed that no one wanted to send their daughters to a single-sex school in a crumbling castle. Those conditions whittled my class down to just thirty-five girls, with me now the only Jew.

There I was, a three-times-a-day-praying, kosher-eating, Sabbath-observing girl. I set myself apart by wearing the skirt of the Mount's navy-blue polyester uniform two inches longer than everyone else's. I was exempt from wearing the school emblem on my blazer, a thick ornate patch of cloth that displayed a cross inside a crown.

At the Mount, it became quickly apparent that I had stumbled into a shocking social experiment. I thought I had prepared myself by reading

My Name Is Asher Lev, Chaim Potok's novel of a Hasidic Jew, an artistic genius, who is so enchanted with religion in general that he paints a picture of the crucifixion. I knew about the outside influences that tempted Asher Lev, and vowed to avoid the traps of overly engaging with those who weren't Jewish. I, too, would avoid having a parallel life, and went to the Mount vowing not to talk to my classmates, certain that I would last no more than two weeks.

Strangely enough, the Mount—shabby, vaguely religious—came to suit me. The sisters tolerated me *shuckling* back and forth (a word derived from Yiddish that literally means to shake) in Hebrew prayer during study hall. They didn't question me when I wrote out the Hebrew letters *bet, samech, dalet* in the right-hand corner of my homework, an acronym for "With God's Help."

Above all, the Mount of my day had a reputation for taking in wayward girls. I, too, was one of them, as I no longer belonged to any community. Instead of being with Chanas and Rahels and Shoshanas, I was now with Maureens, Marys, and Theresas, names that were completely disorienting to me, names that indicated I had landed in a different universe. My parents had accomplished their goal—they had successfully cut me off from my Orthodox community, never thinking I might end up attracted to Catholicism instead.

A few months into school, I made friends, but spiritual confusion rained down on me. I sat out chapel services and religion classes with the handful of Protestants in my class, wondering what my salvation would look like. Would it be with the Lubavitcher rebbe's followers, or with the vibrant young nuns who wore jeans and took students on camping trips? With whom did I prefer to connect? Both groups, as polar opposite as they seemed, offered close-knit community—and I wanted to belong somewhere, anywhere. Still, I was silent and jittery when classes began each day with a prayer in Jesus's name and blessed by the sign of the cross. In those moments, I was an anomaly, an oddity.

When Andrea invited me to her sweet sixteen for a Friday night, I was flattered, relieved to be wanted, and yet scared. It would be my first Shabbat outing since arriving at the Mount. The summer Sabbath days ahead looked long and draining, making my Jewish-tinged rebellion feel stale and inconsequential. Andrea's party was an opportunity to start anew at the Mount and in my life.

Riding in the car to her house that Friday night was like learning to walk again after a long confinement. The oncoming headlights of the cars were too bright. The piles of pasta and pizza at the party overwhelmed me—yet I stayed at the house on Oxbow Circle in Wethersfield, stayed right through the panic I was sure my sin had fueled. I stayed until I realized that I was having a good time, that I finally had friends, that I had broken the stalemate between my parents and me. I stayed because I finally felt free of rules and the despair that came with trying to navigate a religious identity about which I had always been unclear.

Given my penchant for glomming onto anyone who would take me away from my unhappy household, it's not surprising that I turned my attention to the kinder, progressive, pant-suited nuns at the Mount. By my final year, I starred in the traditional senior class skit, "The Twelve Days of Christmas," as the partridge, dressed from head to toe in the brown polyester I had borrowed from Sister Pam, the dean of students. Sister Constance, the physics teacher, made my aerodynamic wings from grocery bags. There were only thirty-five of us for the seventy-nine parts detailed in the song, so Andrea did a quick turn-around from playing one of the three French hens to one of the six geese a-laying. Denise, a tall sweet girl, was my pear tree. I saw no reason not to participate, as there was not a single word in the song about Jesus.

My fantasies about converting to Catholicism were short-lived, as Christmas remained the one crucial custom that separated me from the sisters and from my classmates. Despite my maternal family's warm history with nuns—our superstitious belief that seeing three of them together dressed in habits brought mounds of good luck—Christmas was just not meant to be my holiday.

My mother agonized over the small silver Christmas tree on my Aunt Gladys's coffee table. "What kind of family did I marry into?" she screamed at my father. Christmas, more so than Easter, separated us from those who weren't Jewish and from my father's family.

When word got out that I did not celebrate Christmas, my classmates fell into two camps: Some felt genuinely sorry for me, as my parents had sorely deprived me of the best day of the year. Others thought I had sadly lost touch with reality. At least Andrea had some idea of what was going on with me, because her parents had Jewish friends and she understood that, like milk and meat, Christmas and Hanukkah did not mix.

Almost three decades after I graduated from the Hebrew Academy, as I flipped through my old prayer book the night before my father's funeral, I was still obsessed with how to express my faith. There was a fairytale quality to the idea of reciting the Kaddish every day that appealed to me. The fantasy and lore of the prayer brought me back to the magical thinking with which I navigated the shoals of childhood and my high school years. There was a feeling bubbling up inside that I needed to recite the daily prayer of remembrance to bring my father back to me, to somehow speak with him and figure him out, even though he was no longer alive. The Kaddish I planned to say would be based as much on grief as it was on unfinished business. By that point, I had not had a real conversation with him in almost a decade. During the darkest period of his illness, I had been launching a life as a newlywed, and then as a new mother. The Parkinson's had robbed him of his voice. The dementia had jumbled his mind and hopelessly scrambled his random memories. He was gone—buried with the secrets I was sure he had. I had been missing my father for so many years; could I make up for the gulf that existed between us by reciting the Kaddish after his death?

In Judaism there is a maxim that if one does a good deed enough times, the feeling of satisfaction will eventually come. "Do the deed and the feeling will follow," my rabbi instructed.

I resolved to say the Mourner's Kaddish for my father for thirty days.

CHAPTER 7

The Kaddish Project

Prayer during that grief-soaked first month of mourning was rote. Awkward. I had taken on the obligation of saying the Kaddish before realizing I had forgotten how to pray. A professor in college who gave me a C on a paper about *Ulysses* said I was like a blind woman trying to describe a painting in front of her, and that's how it initially felt saying the traditional prayer of mourning.

I was grateful that Judaism had a contingency plan of prayer on a schedule for the faith-impaired like me.

Among the mourners at the daily egalitarian minyan of ten men and women in my temple was a friend who was nearing the end of eleven months of saying Kaddish for her father. Sarah helped me with the choreography of when to stand, bow, and sit during the service. She sensed when I lost my place and pointed out where we were in the prayer book.

Even when I found my place in the text, Hebrew was the starchy language of formal prayer, an obstacle to approaching my father in his afterlife. I stumbled through words in which I was once fluent, barely pronouncing a semblance of them, with no idea of what I was actually saying until I glanced at the translation on the left side of the prayer book. The Aramaic language of the Kaddish was rooted in an ancient world, and I worried the words until they were a tangled, mangled mess.

The same Kaddish—five short paragraphs, each punctuated by an "amen"—occurred toward the end of each of the three daily prayer services. The evening service was my favorite because that was the time of day I had felt closest to my father when I was little, when he often came to my room to observe the night sky from my window in the midst of bad weather. "Storms always come in from the south," he taught me, "and this one will be a doozy." I equated snowstorms with my father's strength. Our house at 1735 Asylum was on a corner with a lot of sidewalk to shovel, and on a snowy day I watched him clear the driveway and sidewalks and come back inside invigorated by the outdoors and the exercise.

With my month of daily prayer, I tried to make a place for myself as a daughter mourning her father. I wanted to assert my right to say the Kaddish as a way to fill in the gaps of silence, the gaps in the love I was sure my father and I had together.

My recitation of a daily Kaddish felt, however, Sisyphus-like. After all, there is not a single instance in the Old Testament where a father declares his love for a daughter. Only the five daughters of Zelophehad in the Book of Numbers do more than fade into history or disappear altogether as they assert their right to inherit their father's parcel in the Holy Land. I think of them as an early inspiration for women who once had to assert their right to inherit the Kaddish as a spiritual practice and personal expression of grief.

For most of Jewish time, the Kaddish was patriarchal. The demarcation was clear: Sons said Kaddish. Daughters did not. The custom goes back to the Talmudic dictum that women are not bound to fulfill commandments that take time away from raising children and keeping house. I also now raised children and kept house, but unlike in my old Jewish day-school days, the Kaddish was my privilege after a sea change that liberalized Judaism. While some women as far back as the seventeenth century loopholed their way to saying the Kaddish, at home they were otherwise mute, at worst, or relegated to the back of the synagogue.

That is why I love the story of Henrietta Szold, the daughter of a rabbi and founder of Hadassah. The oldest child in a family of eight daughters and no sons, Szold declined a male friend's offer to say Kaddish in her stead when her mother died in 1916. "The Kaddish means to me that the survivor publicly manifests his wish and intention to assume the relation to the Jewish community that his parents had, and that the chain of tradition remains unbroken from generation to generation," she wrote. "You can do that for the generation of your family. I must do that for generations of my family."[1] In the mid-twentieth century, Rabbi Joseph Soloveitchik, a primary figure in Modern Orthodox Judaism, ruled that a woman could say the Kaddish on her own if a minyan of men was present.

By the end of that first month I was a regular among the mourners at the evening minyan, and I started to master the words of the Kaddish. My fluency came near Thanksgiving, in a rush of deeper understanding. I finally began to read the words in the prayer book with meaning, with *kavanah,* intention.

I was praying.

Looking back on my determinative Kaddish project, I understand the prayer's theology in a new way. With the help of the insights of Rabbi Elie Kaunfer, a Conservative rabbi and liturgist who heads Hadar, a progressive institute of Jewish learning, I learned that Kaddish is not a prayer of automatic or unreasonable praise for a God demanding adoration in the midst of a devastating loss. Rabbi Kaunfer asserts that the Kaddish prayer transforms "from a testimony to faith in a God whose actions cause us to suffer for reasons we don't understand, to a prompt that reminds God of the brokenness of the world."[2]

The prayer's first words, "Magnified and sanctified be His great name," are simply a request for God to be honored and adored. This resonated so much with me and, to my mind, this insight put forward a modest God, a caring God, a God who suffers with His people and is willing to earn the honor of acquiring a great and eternal name from His people.

While much has been said about how the Kaddish does not say a single word about death, neither is God's name mentioned in the prayer. As

---

1   Jewish Women's Archive, Henrietta Szold to Haym Peretz, September 16, 1916, https://jwa.org/media/henrietta-szold-s-letter-to-haym-peretz-on-saying-kaddish-for-her-mother.

2   My Jewish Learning, Rabbi Elie Kaunfer, "The Mourner's Kaddish Is Misunderstood," https://www.myjewishlearning.com/article/the-mourners-kaddish-is-misunderstood/.

Rabbi Kaunfer notes, "God will only be made great and holy at the end of days, when all nations recognize God as the supreme moral force in the world."[3] The Kaddish's refrain expresses a wish: "May His great Name be blessed forever and for all eternity." But we are not there yet. We aspire, we hope, in the shadow of a shattering death, for which we say the Kaddish.

The Kaddish is radical in that in the midst of our grief, the prayer dares us to imagine a world significantly better than the one in which we live. God is with us; He is yearning alongside us. With this new perspective on the theology of the Kaddish, I was no longer angry with God; perhaps He loved me despite my spiritual struggles.

I watched many sunsets through the chapel's domed skylight—not only watching day turn into night but, as Jewish law dictates, I witnessed the sun go down to bring forward a new calendar day. There was renewal in darkness. The daily minyan had a way of pulling me in, creating a structure for engaging with my father—something I had not had when he was alive.

Soon after her own father died, my mother had looked up from correcting school papers late one night and swore she saw him next to her playing dominos at our kitchen table, his white linen *guayabera* shirt crisp and pristine. I stared at the skylight for a month of evenings, hoping and praying that I would see my father as clearly as she had seen hers, as clearly as I had when I was flailing underwater in Felipe's aluminum pool. I wanted my father to look down at me in his Sherlock Holmes deerstalker hat or, when it was very cold, his blue and white cap emblazoned with the large *Y* for Yale.

"See what I'm doing for you, Dad." He had to know that I was devoting my days to remembering him, and not just within the structure of a prayer service. I looked for him in my rearview mirror. I hoped he would peer around the corner in my hallway. I thought it more likely that he might appear to me at night. In life, we had connected in the darkest

---

3   Kaunfer, "Mourner's Kaddish."

hours of the morning as he watched storms from my window or sat with me when I was feverish or asthmatic. In those middling thirty days of the Kaddish, I waited for my father, waited for him to give me some sort of sign, waited for us to engage in a celestial conversation. He would tell me all. However, my father did not do the equivalent of sitting down with me to play dominoes. His mysteries had not unlocked for me.

I needed more time. I decided to say Kaddish for the entire eleven months after all.

During that year, would I transmogrify into a temple-going, nonpraying, selectively kosher, nonfasting, skeptical, superstitious, terrified, brazen, monotheistic, mezuzah-kissing, idol-worshipping Jew?

Working a year of Kaddish into my life, determined not to skip a single day, was challenging, often overwhelming. It required the patience and cooperation of my family, which now included a young son, Adam. My husband traveled constantly for work.

There were other factors I couldn't control, such as ensuring there was the prerequisite number of ten men and women, the required minyan that was said to offset the isolation of grief, before we could hold the service. Sometimes nine of us waited for a tenth, which made me anxious. I was on a quest and needed a minyan to help me get there.

I minyan-hopped too. While Temple Emanuel in Newton, Massachusetts, was my home base, I wanted to keep up my daily routine, not miss a day trying to engage with my father. I widened my search for different minyans so that I never had to pause on my Kaddish journey of getting closer to my father to uncover his secrets. Some synagogues were closer to me or fit my schedule better; others were more reliable in raising a minyan.

At Orthodox synagogues, sunset determines the timing of evening services, which can begin early in winter. Kehillith Moshe, one such Orthodox synagogue in a nearby Boston suburb that I sometimes attended during the winter for convenience and out of curiosity, I found that among so many men my voice was shaky and pitched too low, especially when I found myself all alone in the women's section. Women were welcome to say the Kaddish at Kehillith Moses as long as they remained behind a divider, a makeshift curtain that made me claustrophobic.

At Kehillith Moses, I agreed to cover my head with a scarf. The other women who occasionally joined me kept hats in the cloakroom. I often had to wait for a tenth man to show up so that I could say the Kaddish because, as a woman, I didn't count for the purposes of a minyan.

One afternoon, I thought I heard Dad whisper to me, "This is not what I want." I was halfway through my year of saying Kaddish and wondered whether I was saying the prayer in spite of what he wanted, as if I had read the letter he sent me that time instead of burning it. I had been waiting to catch a glimpse of him after his death but all I got was this chiding, that perhaps I was more fixated on the undertaking or the end goal rather than being genuinely devout or creating a posthumous relationship with him. Was I simply returning to a version of my former, and compulsive, religious behavior?

On a night when the timing was tight to get to my nightly recitation, I made an abrupt U-turn on broad, highly trafficked Harvard Street in Brookline, Massachusetts. No sooner had I done so than a police officer flashed his lights and put on his siren to pull me over. Time was evaporating and I was starting to panic as he went through the motions of verifying my license.

"Get back in your vehicle," the officer broadcast from his cruiser as I walked over to rap on his window.

"Can we get on with this?" I asked. "I need to get to a religious service." Up to that point my attendance had been perfect. I was afraid that skipping a night would reset me back to zero.

"Back to your car now!" said the officer. Arms crossed, I stood stock-still. Saying Kaddish in the eyes of God for my father was certainly more important than obeying these petty, man-made rules.

"Hands on the hood so I can see them."

"You don't understand," I yelled. "I have to get to the synagogue to pray for my father. Don't you have a father? I did, and he's gone now. I need to get to synagogue to remember him, to honor him."

The officer stared at me, wide-eyed, during this outburst. "You got anyone to go home to?" he asked quietly.

"I do," I whispered.

He didn't give me a ticket. I arrived at minyan just five minutes late.

"You're overdoing it," was my mother's assessment when she found out I was still saying the Kaddish past my original goal of thirty days. "You'll never do that for me," she added, the source of her true disappointment.

The Kaddish had begun as a fixation with piecing together who my father really was, with finding my way through to him at last. I was not ready to let go, either of my father or of the prayer.

In my determination not to skip a day of Kaddish, I went searching while on vacation in Rome for a temple among the city's more than nine hundred churches. I found the Great Synagogue, where armed policemen surrounded the courtyard. A private security guard asked my husband, not me, what business he had there. I told the young guard, who was wearing a *kippah*, that I needed to say the Kaddish for my father. "*Americana*," he muttered.

Inside, the daily minyan was like walking into a sepia photograph with the cantor and rabbi wearing traditional robes and hats. Ken and I had to sit separately. A divider, improvised with a row of tall potted plants as severe as the policemen outside, walled off the women, who talked throughout the service until I rose to say the Kaddish.

As I stood, the woman next to me put a hand on my arm that was much gentler than Abuela had done all those years ago. "Ladies don't have to," she whispered.

I gently removed her hand. "I want to," I said.

During my year of Kaddish I broke out of the role of passive mourner. It began to happen at Kehillath Israel in Brookline, a traditional Conservative synagogue whose congregants—most of them regulars who went just to be part of a minyan so that people could say Kaddish—raced through the evening service, practically humming their entreaties to God. It was an express train of a service.

The basement chapel looked like an old-world yeshiva. Many of the congregants were elderly and some arrived with caregivers. This old-style worship service was where I became proficient in the evening service. No one announced page numbers. There were no breaks between sections in the liturgy. The more time I spent there, the more I admired the minyan members for standing despite their challenges as they recited the Amidah—the standing prayer that is said before the second recitation of the Kaddish in the service. The praying began with a jangle of voices that sounded like loose change in a pocket. Canes crashed to the floor as this minyan stood and bowed together. By the time we said the Kaddish the second of two times in the service, our voices were one.

I learned the order of the daily evening service, called *ma'ariv*, from the first significant word in the opening blessing of the evening service. Its etymology rooted in the Hebrew word *erev*, which means evening. *Ma'ariv* is a version of the word that functions as a verb, which means "to bring on night."

I asked the ritual director of my synagogue to make a tape for me of the service. I picked up the chanting the same way I learned to play the violin as a child—mimicking the music I heard on a record. I listened to the tape in the car as Adam, then five years old, drifted off to sleep in the back seat. As I practiced for a solid month, many of the prayers came back to me from my Hebrew Academy days.

By the time I was ready to conduct services as one of the more senior mourners in the minyan, I had the Kaddish memorized. On January 19, 2003, what would have been my father's eighty-fourth birthday, I led the ma'ariv service for the first time at minyan. I was thrilled to learn the order of the service, thrilled to be leading the Kaddish. Thrilled to feel as if I were getting closer to my father, even in death.

I thought I saw my father one time that year when I woke with a start and glimpsed his back at the door of my bedroom, wearing an old cashmere coat he'd inherited from Grandpa and his trademark deerstalker hat. He lingered a few seconds before vanishing. The sighting reminded me of a midrash—a story or commentary on a text from the of Torah—that I learned at the Hebrew Academy. Moses was the only human in history to glimpse God, and when he did he only saw the back of God's head. Maybe ghostly sightings by the living are actually glimpses of the Divine. God transforms himself into the image of our beloved dead in a prayer that does not include a single word about death—a prayer that is solely a paean to the Almighty's power. Had I seen God or my father? Were they now one and the same for me?

I sat up for a while feeling elated, waiting for my father to return, but as much as I tried to will myself to see him, he never directly appeared to me.

After the full eleven months, the Kaddish had failed me, and failed my father.

CHAPTER 8

The Ninety-Day Wonder

The master's thesis that I had so much trouble finishing while at the Columbia School of Fine Arts in the mid-1980s was a thinly veiled collection of short stories about my father called "The Ninety-Day Wonder." Many of these stories portrayed him as awkward, occasionally cranky, and always secretive—so much so that even when he told me about the war years he was careful not to make himself a character in his own stories. It's obvious to me now why I had so much trouble filling the gaps in my father's history.

The title story dealt with the time K. Harold Bolton entered the Navy as a Ninety-Day Wonder, which I thought meant he was extraordinary, but would later find out is a pejorative term for college-educated officer candidates who were fast-tracked for the war effort. In the summer after his 1940 graduation from Yale, when he was twenty-one, my father trained at the Officer Candidate School in the Brooklyn Navy Yard for just three months, a highly accelerated program that concluded with men who had socks older than my father having to salute him as an officer, albeit a junior one.

The thesis was my first organized effort at understanding my father, and it didn't go so well. That was when my long-time boyfriend Michael had drifted away and I was still living in an isolated, cheerless room at the Y. I had a secretarial job at the Jewish Theological Seminary, the seat of Conservative Judaism, that took up most of my time and where

I began to experience religion in a way that comfortably rested between tradition and modernity. The first woman rabbi had been ordained at the seminary a year before I arrived; there was some disagreement between traditionalists and progressives over the validity of her *s'micha*—literally, a laying on of hands, the very spirituality of a rabbinic ordination.

At the seminary I dated sweet-natured rabbinical students who invited me to the movies or to Shabbat dinners in their dorm rooms. I sat through the film *Shoah* twice with two different aspiring rabbis, one of whom asked how I felt about moving to Israel. Unlike my mother, who had begged her great love Manuel to take her with him, to me Israel was an ancient abstract, a place of stone and calamity.

My thesis languished another year, prompting my father to make a rare phone call in which he told me: "Finish, or live with the fact that you have done everything to get your degree except the damn master's dissertation."

The university as well had a punitive attitude. If I didn't complete my thesis I'd forever be branded ABD—All But Dissertation—in the academic community and, more important, in my father's mind. A failure. A nothing. A Bad Daughter, another sort of ABD.

I cranked out my thesis by my father's deadline, albeit two semesters later than my graduating class—which meant picking up my diploma from a specially designated room where I was handed my degree unceremoniously. I walked out into the broad sunlight with a piece of paper in hand, the tangible result of my anticlimactic accomplishment.

I didn't intend to be a secretary forever. The next month I had a job interview at the Anti-Defamation League in New York that my father arranged for me with the help of his cousin and family elder, Abbot Rosen. Abbot had been the head of the organization's Chicago office for over forty years, his first and only job out of Columbia Law School. He lived with his wife and grown daughter in a Frank Lloyd Wright House in Hyde Park, around the corner from Louis Farrakhan—who, I would come to learn, was understandably the subject of several thick files in Abbot's organization.

Abbot was fleetingly famous when a group of Nazis acquired a legal permit to march in the predominantly Jewish Chicago suburb of Skokie. Carl Reiner played him in a television movie as the stoic head of the Jewish civil rights organization who revered the First Amendment and acknowledged that, no matter how odious, Nazis had a right to free speech. This was 1980, and my father was so excited about Reiner's portrayal of his cousin that he brought a portable television to my dorm room so I wouldn't miss it.

My job at the ADL included a special mail run that I made every Thursday. From the pickup spot at the Chrysler Building, I'd slog four avenues back to my office hauling two heavy sacks of hate mail and periodicals addressed to one Mr. John Windsor—a fictitious name my boss used to subscribe to homegrown newspapers and other correspondence from right-wing extremist groups. I kept track of domestic hate groups mostly through what I gleaned from Mr. Windsor's mail.

Beginning in 1987, I monitored these fringe groups alongside a motley group of office mates, some of whom had been in the research department since God separated the earth from the waters. Where once I had read novels and short stories by my classmates at Columbia, I now read mimeographed hate rags inked in purple, ungrammatical newspapers that turned my fingers sooty, and crude invitations to Ku Klux Klan rallies and white supremacist gatherings. Within six months of my stint on the right-wing desk, I was one of the country's foremost experts on the KKK and neo-Nazis. I knew more about those closed groups than I did about my family.

An entire crew of women, very much mid-century in look and manner, brought me dilapidated, bulging research files, in which I highlighted names and meeting dates. It felt strange to be the de facto boss of women who were my mother's age. Mildred, the most vocal of them, asked, "What's a nice girl like you doing keeping track of these *vildechai*—these wild animals? Like I tell my daughter, don't be so fussy; get married!"

But keep track I did. I published my findings in reports that I wrote for the FBI and the Bureau of Alcohol, Tobacco, and Firearms. The extremists eventually learned my name, and it both thrilled and terrified me when they wrote me up in their hate screeds. According to them, I was a puppet of ZOG, the Zionist Occupied Government. I was a tricky little Jewess who made up lies for a living.

I had a counterpart who kept track of left-wing activities—a toupee'd, middle-aged poet, thirty years older than I. He was fascinated by elderly Jewish Communists and mostly reported on those die-hard octogenarians on oxygen and in wheelchairs. He went to bedraggled meetings of the Communist Party on his own time. He and I were saving America from extremists, but the divide between the ragtag band of gleeful haters I monitored and the limping elderly Communists on whom my colleague spied was this: the former hated Jews and the latter were mostly Jews. While the left-wing expert was passionate about teasing hate from ambiguity, my guys (and they were almost all men) were straightforward: Jews and Blacks were the devil's spawn. Alarming numbers of illegal immigrants were contributing to the extinction of the white man in America. The Jews staged the Holocaust to milk world sympathy and provide an excuse for the State of Israel. All of it was too ridiculous to contemplate, until it wasn't—until I realized that one day these people could seep into the mainstream and poison it.

There was a particular method to the nonautomated madness of the research department's daily operation. It was madness as thick as the glue the bent-over clerks used to mount articles that they filed away in the department's library. I furiously underlined pertinent names and events in every hatemonger publication to which Mr. Windsor subscribed, and the articles were then filed. For example, if I tagged six names or subjects in an article, each merited its own file. These could be anything from names like David Duke to subjects like Holocaust Denial. Down the hall, my coworker was losing his mind over Louis Farrakhan and Lyndon LaRouche.

Mortimer Rosenbaum, who sat at a desk outside my office, was one of my favorites in the department. Mortimer was an enigma. He hated every moment of the forty years he had spent working for the organization, but when he finally retired as a researcher he had nowhere to go. He wound up, post-retirement, back in the department, where cutting and pasting articles gave his days shape and purpose. A large man, he wedged himself into his desk and he rarely got up once settled in. He worked the glue brush and scissors as if he had paws instead of opposable thumbs. His murmured phone calls frequently drifted around the corner and into my office with its secrets. "I don't want to get AIDS," he whispered into the receiver. He spelled out the acronym AIDS in Hebrew letters—*aleph, yud, dalet, samech*—confident that he had created a code no one could crack.

Beneath his brown-tinted aviator glasses, Mortimer teared up the day he confessed that he never took public transportation. It turned out that he and I shared the same secret—we both had panic disorder. He had experienced a panic attack in a crowded subway car two decades earlier, and since then had only taken taxis. "Because of the taxis, I can't afford to go anywhere for fun, so I think of the taxi rides themselves as little pieces of vacation," he said.

"Mortimer is not a good role model for you," the therapist I went to see about my panic attacks said. Unlike Mortimer Rosenbaum, who could avoid his panic simply by staying aboveground, I could not avoid the night.

The first time I had a panic attack, I was sleeping next to my boyfriend, Michael, when surges of adrenaline and waves of panic suffocated me. I was afraid to wake him, so I rocked back and forth in bed as if in prayer until the sun came up, and then I dry-heaved the rest of the day.

The panic attacks were exhausting and hiding them from Michael, more so. I desperately wanted to be the perfect girlfriend: composed and supportive. Above all, I tried to will myself to be strong. I could not tell my boyfriend how disabled I felt. The middle-aged woman who saw me when I secretly went for help at the counseling center on campus did not try to disabuse me of the notion that I was insane. "Some women have babies to ease their anxiety," she said, rather ominously.

Like many people with panic disorder, I catastrophized about the future. What would become of me? Would Michael finally see that I was too crazy to be the mother of his children? I'd end up locked in the mental institution to which my mother claimed I was destined—which wouldn't have been a surprise, since melancholy and craziness ran on both sides of my family. My mother seemed unhinged, even delusional. Grandma Bolton's brother, Barney the doctor, hospitalized her in the 1930s for hysterical outbursts and suicidal thoughts. They treated her with shock therapy back when the protocol was still in its infancy; she and my grandfather never shared a bedroom after that. Through the scrim of memory, I see my grandfather in a bowtie and plastic apron washing dishes for my grandmother, who forever suffered a bout of this or a spell of that.

When I worked at ADL, I was only beginning to realize how panic had always been intrinsic to my life. My mother's terror of flying was why family vacations had exclusively been road trips, which my father meticulously planned with the help of Triple A maps and guidebooks. I was in charge of looking up the towns we drove through and reading out loud about places with odd little museums dedicated to minutiae like thimbles and yarn and buttons. I found breweries and wineries that made under-the-radar beer and wine.

People tried to help me shake off the panic. Aunt Reina took me shopping at Caldor for some retail therapy. Michael's mother, a large, pale woman with a lacquered-blonde bouffant hairdo, pancake makeup, and thick red lipstick, took me to lunch and told me to find beauty in nature. I had thought of her as the mother I always wanted, but in the end she and I were competitors vying for her son's unconditional love. At least no one threw me fully clothed into a cold shower, as they had done one time to my grandmother; but the panic continued, and at the end of my sophomore year of college I wound up collapsed in the emergency room with depression and anxiety. I was sure that I was just days away from the psychiatric facility. A girl I went to high school with happened to be the intake clerk that night. "What happened to you, Miss Salutatorian?" she said. "How did you get to be such a mess, girl?"

My father sat next to me with his head in his hands.

I had been on this high-stress, high-secrecy job for a year when my father came to visit me at work. By then, Dad and I had become friends of a sort.

He was less stern, even friendly. He was happy to accompany me on my mail drop to the Chrysler building.

"This is very special mail I'm picking up," I told him, trying to impress.

"I'm happy to have the exercise," was all he said.

I wanted to tell him that he was not the only person who carefully handled secrets in our family. I wanted to ask him about so many things, including his letter that I had burned.

As we walked past Tudor City he told me that after the war he had dated a girl who lived in one of the stately brick apartment buildings there. He looked for the bars to which he had taken dates. "Things change," he said wistfully.

What things, I wondered? He was starting to list to one side when he walked. In his profile I thought I saw his loneliness. He wore a suit that had belonged to his father; the arms were too short and the jacket didn't button.

At the Chrysler Building, he paused. "I'll wait in the lobby," he said.

"Aren't you coming up with me?" I wanted to show him how I collected the fictitious John Windsor's mail. "This is an elaborate spy operation in action!"

"It's *your* mission," he said, and I noticed that he used the word *mission*.

"You're not even curious?"

"I'm respectful."

"But I'm a detective in this job," I prodded.

"You certainly were a nosy little girl."

That was rich, coming from someone who refused to discuss those extended vacations in Guatemala "to visit friends," friends he never introduced us to or discussed or even named. I had written an entire thesis about him—biographical fiction sprinkled with the few facts I had gleaned, such as how he had done a stint as an accountant for the United Fruit Company on one of his jaunts. "But wasn't that a well-known CIA front?" I asked, excited at the possibilities. "I was an accountant," he merely said.

There was still so much I didn't know—except that, already in his seventies, his Parkinson's symptoms were gathering momentum. It would be the last trip my father would make to New York to suss out what was happening with me.

"Your father is genteel," Mortimer observed when I returned to work. "But he has sad eyes."

"He does, Mortimer."

I closed the door to my office to sort John Windsor's mail and cried.

CHAPTER 9

The Somnambulists

There was a time when King Solomon, the wisest of men, could not tell day from night. The Queen of Sheba tricked him into believing that night went on forever by hanging above his bed a black tapestry woven with diamond stars and pearly planets. When Solomon awoke in the morning he thought it was still night, and slept on.

If I could have made a magical tapestry like Sheba's, I would have used it to soothe my father into believing all was well. It would have depicted night on the Pacific Ocean—waves gently rolling, the moon offering guidance from the bridge of his supply ship.

I liked my father best in the deepest of night when he lulled me to sleep, narrating the weather or describing the constellations. But a few hours later I, his somnambulist child, appeared at the threshold of his bedroom. Once a somnambulist himself, he knew not to rouse me from my sleepwalker's twilight. He closely tracked me, his flashlight pointed to the floor. My episodes of sleepwalking were always followed by bouts of amnesia. But if I had a recurring somnambulist dream, it was likely the one where I jumped from the top of the basement stairs, waking up before I cracked my head open on the damp, cold squares of yellow-beige-red flooring.

Another form of sleepwalking continued for my father and me throughout my adolescence and young adulthood. We tiptoed around each other, careful not to startle one another. Afraid to rouse the other from our entrenched places. Afraid to disturb each other's dreams.

On blue-black nights when my asthmatic coughing shook the house, my father was a sentry at my bedroom window, gazing out, in the expansive night. What did he see? All that was out there were fields that belonged to Saint Joseph College, where many Mounties went to college. But he stood at attention in his mismatched pajamas, a posture he affected so that he could still graze a chart at five foot seven, the minimum height for an officer. Decades after he'd been in the Navy, I understood that the war was always with him. He had never really left the bridge of his supply ship. From that location he said he fished out dead bodies half-eaten by sharks in the Pacific. He watched General MacArthur wade ashore in the Philippines. The horizon was my father's blank screen, and it served as a gateway to adventure, to daydreaming, to peace. I felt that he missed his former life of excitement, of participating in something important like running guns and butter in the war. But in his civilian life there was always the adrenaline rush of tracking weather.

My father believed that sailors lived and died according to how well prepared they were for the weather, a belief that colored the seasons of my childhood. On summer nights, he stood on the porch to observe lightning and listen for thunder. He paced during storms like a distracted maestro, doing a somnambulist-like loop through the kitchen, living room, and dining room, and shouting out emergency rules as lightning cracked the sky and lit the world the color of steel: "No telephone, no television, no showering! If we have to, we go directly to the car. A car with its rubber tires is the safest place to be during an electrical storm. In the event of a tornado warning we shelter in the basement."

I was that little girl who worried. I lived in dread of lightning striking the house as Dad rushed outside to sit in the Malibu. The car never moved an inch off the driveway. On those wind-howling nights, full of electricity, he belted us three kids together in the backseat; the silver buckle pressed against my belly, making it as hard to breathe as if I were having an asthma attack.

When the Connecticut winters set me off on a coughing jag, my father filled the glass bowl of my humidifier every hour to keep it whistling like a teakettle. My bedroom, smelling of Ben-Gay, was as humid as my mother's tropics. But with all my father's directions and warnings about staying warm and hydrated and still beneath my bedcovers, I worried that I would never catch the breath trapped in my mentholated chest. I developed a fear of lightning. Any window-rattling storm signaled an emergency to Dad, and now to me, too.

My father's obsession with the horizon reminds me of yet another midrash. This one is about Adam staring at a limitless vista until he could see directly into the future. When K. Harold Bolton saw millions of twinkling stars from the bridge of his supply ship, did he glimpse the children he would one day have? Did he see himself perched at my window, the one that looked onto Asylum Avenue, the hub of my universe, where I watched the traffic churning by day and the expansive fields of Saint Joseph College under the black-stained sky of night? Did he see his future self, observing the weather and monitoring my breathing—or did he see himself as merely an outline in the midnight steam, unable to protect me from illness or from my mother?

Whenever snow bleached the world, my father went into hyperstorm mode. His self-styled deployment, to battle heavy weather and the bad colds that stemmed from it, included doubling the dose of the chewable Zestabs that colored my tongue red, and of Acerola, the intense, tangy disc of vitamin C whose tartness made my mouth water. Every morning Carol and I wrapped the vitamins in our napkins to flush them down the toilet. One time, the Zestab stayed at the bottom of the bowl, bleeding out cherry red, and my father fished it out to show us. "Did you think you'd get away with this?" he demanded.

My father's storm protocol also extended to waterproofing our boots atop old issues of *The Hartford Times* and wearing the bearish coat he kept for the blusteriest of days, a coat similar to the one he had worn while stationed in Greenland. He bought this successor at the Groton Naval Base in Connecticut, where he also acquired very sensible shoes, and thick gloves that made his hands go stiff. He loved the Groton Naval

Base; each time he took us to the Officer's Club for dinner he was crisply saluted, as if he had stepped into a time machine where for an hour or two he could recoup a few privileges from his former life.

After my year of saying the Kaddish, I sent for my father's naval records. I already knew him to be the bravest man in the world, but I hoped to read more into the black-and-white image of him taken below deck as a young officer. When I lived in my first apartment, I had that picture mounted in a handsome silver frame, and it was only after years of studying it that I realized I could just make out the chain of his dog tags. At the height of my orthodoxy in high school, my father had told me that while in the Navy he declined to identify himself neutrally with an *O* stamped on his dog tags that meant he would accept last rites from any religious tradition. In the military, *O* functioned like the universal blood type, good for almost anyone. Instead, my father opted to have his dog tags stamped with an *H*, which stood for the biblical-sounding descriptor *Hebrew*. I wanted access to more secrets and stories like that one.

My father's Navy records arrived in a thick packet wrapped in brown paper. As I slowly went through them, the information that floated to the top was that he was exceptionally stubborn, inexperienced, and always one of the youngest officers on any ship to which he was assigned. The numerous Reports on the Fitness of Officers in my father's file consistently indicated that although he stood out for his bravery, loyalty, and patriotism, in the end my father was an average, even naïve, officer.

This was not the kind of mystery I had expected to solve. Although I was thrilled to have the status reports, solid evidence that revealed facets of the man, they surprised and ultimately disappointed me. I was so sure these reports would confirm that he was larger than life. Instead, the reports didn't mesh with the man I thought he was. From the few pictures I had seen of him in uniform, I expected an exceptional and capable officer who acted much older than a Ninety-Day Wonder.

Maybe this is the way most children see their parents—through a combined lens of time and story that ultimately fuses into legend. My father was the man who did pushups every morning on the green shag rug of his bedroom. He was the man who walked a brisk two miles a day, even in winter. When I was a child, he expected me to follow his orders exactly as he gave them. And yet, I read in his file a note he had written to his commanding officer on the first Christmas after Pearl Harbor, in which he laid out his reasons for disobeying orders. He had been waiting to ship out in San Francisco, and wrote that he had decided to give the men under his command three additional hours of liberty to boost their morale. His unilateral decision must have incurred a reprimand.

I even came upon an actual punishment for my father. It happened toward the end of the war, when his commanding officer remanded him to quarters for twenty-four hours after he went AWOL for a day. For a man who never actually backed the car off the driveway the many times he threatened to leave my mother, going AWOL didn't seem in character. The information rounded out a profile of an officer who did not follow established ship routines and, according to notations from his commanding officer, did not wish to acquaint himself with them. Nor did he properly learn to use the sextant for navigational calculations. Perhaps it was because those kinds of calculations demystified the heavens, while Lieutenant Bolton preferred to romanticize them.

Over the years, I had seen glimpses of Dad the romantic, who cried when he listened to opera on Saturday afternoons. Dad the patriot listened to John Philip Sousa's crisp, booming marches with his hand over his heart. Dad the accountant finally, reluctantly, learned to follow established routines.

My brother has become the keeper of the Navy stories Dad shared with him alone. John claims that our father was never AWOL. The real story, he says, is that Lieutenant Bolton had fraternized with the ship's Black cook, who like the many men of color who prepared the ship's food was called Cookie. My father had stepped out of class and hierarchy, away from racism and inhumanity, to put his arm around a man who had just received news that his brother had died while fighting in Europe. He called Cookie by his given name, Ernie. The lieutenant also removed his hat in a show of mourning, making him technically out of uniform. Finally, the lieutenant wept with Ernie on the deck of their ship, the USS *Trinity*. For that, he was punished.

Contrary to the jumbled, often discouraging, naval reports, there was a promotion for my father at the end of the war. By the time the Navy honorably discharged Lieutenant Commander Bolton in 1945, I had something akin to jetlag from traveling back in time to his war, to the life he loved before I appeared. But I still didn't feel satisfied.

There was a glimmer of that disciplined naval life of stars and moon on a bright Saturday morning in March 1970 when my father announced that there would be an eclipse that afternoon. I was a big fan of almost anything to do with the infinite universe. I loved the television show *Lost in Space*. I watched the Robinson family in their sleek out-of-this-world skintight suits act unfailingly loving toward one another despite their intergalactic predicament. I was thrilled that the name of the oldest daughter was Judy. Maybe I, too, could be a Robinson, a member of this dream family. Not bound to the Boltons and Alboukreks here on Earth.

As the appointed hour for the eclipse approached, my father ordered us to stay in the den. He explained that the moon would pass over the sun so that, for a moment, day would become night, recalling how the Queen of Sheba's tapestry deceived Solomon. Such an inversion fascinated me. Outside there would be no light, no glare to gauge the intense, prolonged rays emanating from a hidden sun—rays that could burn through our retinas and blind us, as my father reminded us.

To demonstrate the rarity and import of the event, Dad bought us sunglasses at the Finast Supermarket in Bishops Corner; the acronym stood for First National Stores and had cost me points on a spelling test. In my father's world, sunglasses weakened young eyes, and yet here he was adjusting round pink and blue plastic sunglasses atop our noses. I sat in the creaky brown tweed rocker, my feet sticking out at a ninety-degree angle, and shut my eyes tightly until I saw a galaxy of swirling light. Then I opened them narrowly, like the thin beams of light that streamed between the slats of the venetian blinds. My father faced the shaded window, his sunglasses perched on his head, wide-eyed, unafraid of pure light disguised as night.

King Solomon's tapestry would keep us in the eternal night. In the hours that contracted in darkness, I roamed the house entombed in sleep. A tapestry wielding its divine magic unfurled over us as my father followed me, his somnambulist child, to the ends of the earth.

CHAPTER 10

Driving Lessons

My mother never managed to achieve one of the crowning glories of the 1960s American housewife—a driver's license. She was a permanent passenger in life, confined to 1735 Asylum Avenue except by the graces of the local bus, or someone—anyone—ferrying her here, there, and everywhere.

For a while, Sunday meant another one of Mom's trial spins around the empty parking lot of the Finast Supermarket with my sister and brother and me in the back seat.

"Here we go again," said my father with resignation as she did dizzying figure eights, with Carol puking into a plastic orange-sherbet container repurposed for her motion sickness. John, on the other hand, loved the stomach-dropping rush brought on by these practice drives where my mother often lurched or spun out of control while my father drummed his fingers through the window onto the roof of the car—the whoosh of wind adding to the thrill and danger of it all.

Dad oversaw these driving lessons in empty parking lots, never on the road. During what would be my mother's final lesson, she pulled into our garage too close to the concrete spackled wall.

"Put the car in reverse, dammit!" my father yelled.

She confused the turn signal with the gearshift. "*Ay Dios mio*, we're not going anywhere," she fretted while the three of us were eerily quiet in the backseat, our arms around each other. When she finally realized how the car worked, she backed the car out and we kids jerked forward. The car scraped along for a few more inches.

"I've had enough for today," growled my father.

"You don't want me to learn to drive," my mother screamed. "You never wanted me to learn!"

She was correct.

My mother's driving adventures were the stuff of a madcap episode of *I Love Lucy*, Matilde-style. We were the wacky American-Latino family at the intersection of Asylum Avenue and La Callé Mercéd, the street my mother lived on in Old Havana. In our house, the American and Latino roles were reversed: my mother was the zany Cuban, improbably married to a hyper-sensible Ricky who was not a bandleader but an accountant in central Connecticut. Fictional Ricky and flesh-and-blood Harold both had smoking jackets, and wives they tried to keep from living *la vida loca*.

My father must have known Matilde would never learn (nor would he permit her) to drive when he picked out a house that sat on a major bus line. He taped a map of the A1 route on the refrigerator as soon as we moved in, and if a destination was not along that line, we did not go. The situation effectively trapped my mother until she cleverly applied for teaching jobs, all of them along the bus route. That is how she wound up teaching Spanish at the Saint Agnes Home for Unwed Mothers.

I was five when my mother boarded the A1 bus most weekdays for the short ride to the Sisters of Mercy, who ran the Saint Agnes Home on Steele Road. She did not see the irony in being pregnant with John at the time. The sisters founded the place in 1914 and, at its peak just after the Second World War, they housed up to fifty pregnant young women from all over the Northeast. They were "the girls who went away," and they did not leave the grounds until after they gave birth. Saint Agnes was the patron saint of virgins and rape victims, and she declared that Jesus Christ was her husband up to the moment of her beheading; now she watched over girls who lived on Asylum Avenue and Steele Road with their shame and with their Spanish lessons from my mother, who translated for them the aphorisms that Mother Superior chirped: "Girls, girls, girls. Too much kissing leads to so much trouble!"

Working at the Saint Agnes Home oddly enough resonated with my mother, whose parents had been happy to get her away from Havana when she was shamefully unmarried at twenty-two, even though she was resolutely virginal. She was the impetuous daughter whose blustering in favor of Castro caught the attention of the neighborhood watch. She was the bully of the house who made her younger sister miserable for having a serious boyfriend while she did not.

In my mother's world, the girls of Saint Agnes had done the forbidden; but it was confusing for her. My mother was both a flirt and a puritan. She was *la mas linda della familia*, the most beautiful of the family—and also the stern girl who had pushed away the boys who tried to hold her hand. She had said no to Fidel Castro himself, even for just a coffee date! And she refused to discuss with her daughters anything that might happen to them below the waist with a boy. Her dating advice to me in later years was "neck up." Yet, she had both craved and feared the body's impulses, growing up in a society rife with double standards in which boys visited prostitutes as a rite of passage while girls ascended to shaky moral pedestals, expected to remain unapproachable until marriage. "Boys are like animals with urges they can't control," my mother counseled, her green eyes going wide with horror and a bit of wonder.

The Asylum Avenue bus lived up to its name and gave my mother asylum in other ways; it provided opportunities. When I was in elementary school, boarding the 3:20 bus with my mother for my allergy shots was like crossing into another country—this one was mostly populated by Portuguese house cleaners. After they finished cleaning for the ladies of West Hartford, they waited for the A1 at nearly every stop from Bishops Corner to Steele Road. They unwittingly created a vibrant language laboratory for my mother; "*This* is how you learn a language, directly from a native speaker!" My mother was flush with excitement—something I had never seen in her.

"Portuguese reminds me of Ladino," she said. In addition to Spanish, my mother spoke the fifteenth-century Spanish tongue that was leavened with Hebrew and a stew of other Mediterranean languages. In those Portuguese ladies and their rapid-fire talk, she heard strains of her precious Ladino—which, like my mother, survived in surprising ways and unlikely places. "Listen to this," she said, thrilled at her discovery. "*Cadera* means hip in Spanish. Add just one extra *i* as in *cadeira* and it means chair in Portuguese!"

It was because of Ladino that my mother's family landed in Cuba for a generation. In the early 1900s, my abuelos embarked on separate boat trips west from Greece and Turkey, respectively. So much the better that they docked in Cuba; Ladino was the precious baggage they lugged from country to country, century to century. It was the language of my ancient crowd. It was a kitchen language, excitedly and loudly spoken by my mother, my aunt, and my grandmother. "No one is angry," Aunt Reina tried to convince me. "That's how we talk."

It was also a language that rubbed shoulders with the Portuguese of the house cleaners who rode the A1 bus. To befriend these women was natural for my mother. They had the same sort of austere Sephardic Jewish faces—Jews who had been wandering the world since the Inquisition. The *j* sound in Ladino was the same vibrating and zippery sound in Portuguese. There was also a fair amount of Arabic in Ladino, as in the word *mashallah*—May God bless you. At the base of everything were interchangeable Hebrew and Spanish words. But nothing made my mother more furious than when someone described Ladino as the Sephardic version of Yiddish. "We are not *polacos*"—her pejorative term for Eastern European or Ashkenazic Jews. When she was angry with my father, "*gringo*" and "*polaco*" flew from her mouth.

At night, my mother became a class of one, drilling herself with a book called *501 Portuguese Verbs*. "So much like Ladino," she said with admiration. She was joyous in making the linguistic leap. On the bus, the Portuguese ladies flashed gold-tooth smiles at her impressive progress. Her accent was good, too. To me, Portuguese was disorienting, in that it was almost familiar but not quite. It was Spanish spoken in a minor key. The syllables were wide enough for me to fall through and miss entire phrases. The *ue*'s of Spanish, as in *bueno*, flattened down to *o*'s in Portu-

guese, as in *bom*. The Portuguese *a*'s were as long and chilly as our basement in winter.

My mother was a language machine. The more fluent she became,
the more involved she was with her new friends; soon after meeting them
she turned entrepreneurial and became their booking agent. First, she
placed them with people she knew in the neighborhood. Like a game of
telephone, word had gotten around to call my mother to find a reliable
house cleaner. My mother co-opted unused blue books from the night
courses my father taught at the University of Hartford and used them to
keep track of the women's jobs. Even my father helped. "These women are
hard workers," he said. "You have to admire that."

Sometimes I heard my mother say things into the telephone like, "Of
course she's honest." Or, "Call me if she doesn't understand whether to use
Pledge or Windex." There were distress calls from the housekeepers to
translate exactly if their employers wanted them to clean or to fold. And
there was the delicate negotiation of a cash-only business. My mother
never took a cent in commission, seeing herself as a self-styled champion
of these women's rights to a decent wage. It was one of the many paradoxes
my mother exhibited, that she was so focused on money and wanting more
of it, while not taking a dime from the women she helped. "The richer, the
cheaper," she grumbled after many a phone call spent trying to up the ante.

Business expanded to the tony Mountain Road area, and my mother
talked to women who would otherwise never acknowledge her. They had
gotten her name from friends of friends in yet another game of suburban
telephone. "I am not a cleaning woman!" my mother said before hanging
up in a fury one night. "I live in West Hartford, just like you!" She would
only go so far in identifying with her clientele.

For our part, my mother hired her bus mate Adelina to clean 1735
Asylum on Thursdays, so that she was no longer "the maid of the house."
Unlike Abuelo and Abuela, who rarely left their apartment without an
escort, Adelina navigated greater Hartford without understanding
English or even recognizing the alphabet. X marked the spot for her sig-
nature when Dad did her income taxes. She cleaned according to color:
Windex blue for glass, Mr. Clean yellow for floors.

Almost everything we did fascinated Adelina. She was confused about how to fold my father and brother's briefs. She stopped and stared when I used my mother's typewriter, as if I were giving a concert. She once asked me to type her name. *"Boa, boa,"* she marveled. Good, good. I did it several times in a row, and when I gave her the paper she pressed it to her chest as if it were a holy text. In half Spanish and half Portuguese, she pantomimed that she would tell her granddaughter in Portugal about my magical word machine.

Adelina worked for us for almost a decade. In that time, my mother taught her how to sign her name and my father helped her navigate the Social Security bureaucracy. My mother might have been that permanent passenger in life, but teaching herself Portuguese reawakened the same confidence that she had when she went back to school a few years before. My mother thought she could learn anything if given a chance. She expanded her teaching from Saint Agnes to tutor in a few local high schools, although she knew she needed actual teaching credentials to go any further. Back then she was determined to find a way to go back to school like Maria Elena, Felipe's wife. "Ah, Maria Elena—*que mujer*," what a woman, Dad said with admiration. Maria Elena was legendary in my house for driving a two-toned Volkswagen bus with her six kids clear across the Pan-American Highway to visit family in Guatemala. I never understood why my mother was not jealous of Maria Elena's driving skills, her bigger house, and her successful husband.

After Maria Elena went back to college to finish up her undergraduate degree, she went to law school. "Going back to school is the best thing you can do for yourself," she told my mother.

"Who will pay for it?" my mother asked, incredulous.

"Your husband."

My mother enrolled at Trinity College in Hartford in the fall of 1965 when she was seven months pregnant with my little brother. Her first test of will was getting through a foggy, menacing, postpartum year of *Don Quijote de la Mancha*.

Studying the novel became a group effort in our house. *Don Quijote* was the longest book my mother had ever attempted to read. She read much of it to me in the small, square, thickly painted yellow kitchen, with her own commentary slipped in. "*Pobresito* Don Quijote, he was such a dreamer and he suffered so much for it," she said, relating to Cervantes's fictional character.

I loved watching my mother trying to make dinner—she barely knew how to cook and resented having to come up with something for the table every night—as she conjured for me another installment of Don Quijote's adventures with the hapless Sancho Panza and the prostitute Dulcinea. To the fantasist Don Quijote, Dulcinea was the finest of women. She was *dulce*—sweet. In my mom's account, Dulcinea was hapless and *fea*. As Mom stirred canned vegetables and ketchup into a pot of stewing meat, the mixture splattering on the book's pages, she said that Don Quijote's precious library burned. "He was too influenced by his books," she said, as if that also explained our charred dinners, the exoskeletons of which we scraped off Pyrex pans.

All of my mother's schoolbooks had an air of mystery. They came to our house wrapped in brown paper displaying exotic stamps from Spain. The books she ordered from the land of Don Quijote were scattered all over the house, many with pages stuck together that had to be parted with a letter opener. I loved the feel of the books' rough paper, their ragged edges.

The most impressive of them was *The Dictionary of the Royal Spanish Academy*, a doorstopper of a book that came directly from Madrid. Every word of the Spanish language was defined between its marbled brown covers—words waiting to be arranged into the labored term papers, many drafts of which my mother wrote and which ended up as crumpled balls of typing paper on the floor of the dining room.

On Sunday nights, the house was abuzz with the sound of my mother's frenetic typing on the baby blue Smith Corona. The white onionskin paper in the typewriter was as fragile as she was. The return carriage grazed the typewriter's metal teeth at full speed as she attempted to fulfill requirement after requirement for her degree, the house filled with the urgent rhythm of type and return, type and return, in between her frequent crying jags. Type and return until she stopped typing altogether and my father tried his hand at boiling hot dogs or sculpting meatloaf to help her out. Type and return until she finally accumulated five pages of haphazard analysis. She stutteringly typed her way to graduation, where my father issued her final assignment: He felt that if she were going to earn a diploma from an American college, then she finally needed to learn the words to "The Star Spangled Banner," four years after she had already become a United States citizen.

Matilde Bolton with daughters Carol and Judy at her 1969
master's graduation from Trinity College in Hartford.

"*Hay, es muy difícil,*" difficult, harder than reading dense Spanish novels, she complained.

"Even Judy knows the words," said my father.

She devised her own strange mnemonics to the national anthem. "Oh, say can you see" turned into the radio call letters of the Hartford station WTIC: "Oh say TIC." WTIC in Hartford was also of help when she sang, "My country TIC, sweet land of liberty of TIC." She became so frustrated with learning these hymns to America that she counteracted by booming out the Cuban national anthem like a petulant child. "To live in chains is to live in dishonor and ignominy. Hear the clarion call. Hasten brave ones to battle."

"Repeat after me," my mother ordered the three of us. *"En cadenas vivir es morir / en afrenta y oprobio sumidos / del clarin escuchad el sonido / a las armas valientes corred."* That's the anthem I would have sung at my graduation if the University of Havana had stayed open," she said with a breathlessness I recognized as the verge of hysteria.

"The only anthem they're singing down there is 'The Internationale,'" my father yelled.

"Mi querida Cuba," my mother moaned. There once was a beautiful blue and green jewel of an island from which she now was exiled forever. She resented that she had come to have a life in which she had to palm an index card with lyrics about the dying light of some twilight's last gleaming. What did that even mean?

The day of her graduation in 1969, my mother wore a rented cap and gown. The tassel on her mortarboard was as jittery as she was. The new pocketbook that hung off her right arm was a graduation gift from my Bolton grandparents—beige and square, and anchored with her initials in silver. The purse was empty, save for a couple of white, blue-lined 3 x 5 index cards on which my father had written out the words of "The Star-Spangled Banner." She was supposed to read the cards the same way my father once did when he said his wedding vows in transliterated Hebrew.

My mother received her American diploma on a warm day in May when she was finally the person she wanted us to know.

Soon after that, she opened her own bank account and left my father.

CHAPTER 11

Batidos de Mamey

The summer I was nine years old, my mother heard the Cubana siren song to return to her homeland, as transplanted to Miami. Her cousins had fled to Miami Beach—cousins she had not seen since before Castro's ascendancy in 1961. This was to be a nostalgic trip as well as her trial separation from Harold Bolton. The fights had spiraled and crept right up to the border of violence. The police and Aunt Reina often mediated. By the time my mother decided to flee with us to Miami, she was red-hot angry all the time, while my father had settled into a stoic blue sadness. The marriage had drained everyone.

The two of them unfurled a thin cover story over their troubles—that we were heading south to attend a family wedding, but my father could not get away from work. My mother's twenty-four-year-old cousin Roberto was to wed Jeanina, a seventeen-year-old Cubana. The potential there for scandal would have been the stuff of high drama; Roberto's mother, Victoria, would have taken to her bed in grand Jubana style had Jeanina not converted to Judaism in time. My mother floated the legend that on her deathbed, Victoria's mother, La Tía Estér, Abuela's older and once-rich sister, taught Jeanina to bless the Shabbat candles.

These were the people who awaited us in Florida, people I was not looking forward to meeting. I wanted to stay in Connecticut, near my father and my Bolton grandparents. Going so far away terrified me—in no way would this trip be an adventure for me. I was confused and upset as to why my parents couldn't make up. What was different about their fight this time? Why was there such an urgency to flee? How long would we be gone? No one paid attention to my questions or to me.

Flying to Florida was never an option; my mother had not been on an airplane since 1959 when she begged God to spare her life on a turbulent Cubana Airlines flight from Havana to New York. Until the scary, twenty-six-hour train ride down the Eastern Seaboard on the Silver Meteor, our lives had only moved forward in the Chevy Malibu or on the Asylum Avenue bus. "All aboard," called the conductor.

Not everyone came aboard. My father did not join us, and I panicked. Carol, John, and I pressed our faces against the window of our sleeper car, crying and vigorously waving good-bye to Dad. Before we had even pulled out of the station, Carol was motion sick, John was homesick, and I was heartsick. I clung to my Barbie, not knowing when or if I would see my father again. On the platform, he held his straw Panama hat over his heart as if he were sending us off on the strains of the national anthem. He had on the brown and paisley shirt he wore for his twenty-fifth reunion year-book photograph from Yale; five years had passed since the four of us—John was not yet born—posed for that picture on the brown tweed living room couch. Each of my parents claimed a daughter. My mother had pulled her long dark hair back into a chignon. When I look at the picture now, it reminds me of how quickly my parents could go from unsettled to glamorous, furious to loving. "Happily married," my father informed his classmates. "Only self-criticism is that I did it too late in life."

We rolled out of Penn Station, moving away from everything that mattered to me, everything that had engaged me in my young life as a detective. It would be months before I saw my father again.

In Miami, the four of us stepped off the train dizzy and nauseated. A teary-eyed, muumuu-ed and white-sandaled woman ran up to us. "Victoria!" my mother cried, throwing her arms around her cousin.

Victoria broke away from my mother to look over the three of us and quickly declared my sister *la mas linda della familia*. That had been my mother's title and she flashed her jealous green eyes at my sister. My brother was a *diablito*, and I was stuck with the pedestrian *la grande*, the oldest.

"*Oye niña*," Victoria ordered me. "*Me casé* when I was just a little older than you. *Me entiendes*?" I understood immediately. I had heard the story of how Tía Estér forced Victoria to wed Alberto, ten years her senior, when she was just fourteen. She was married off so unbearably young to prevent any number of tragedies that could have sent her father the rabbi to an early grave. She might have fallen in love with a Cubano, a *católico*. She might have been wild and compromised her virtue. A Latina girl's virginity was once an essential part of her dowry; if she lost it, she was unmarriageable to the right boy. When I did the math, I realized I still had five good years before I could be betrothed like Victoria to the wrong man.

I was aware that my father was not with us as we trudged behind the redcaps who loaded our luggage into the trunk of a white Lincoln. Alberto was in the driver's seat and grunted at us. His toupee was loose and he chewed on the wet unlit stub of a cigar. It was hard to believe he was the *mujeriego*, the womanizer, my mother and aunt said he was, that in Cuba Alberto ran around with the women who rolled cigars in his factory. Perhaps it was the wealth he once had that attracted them; before Castro marched into Havana, he and Victoria lived in a large home in Vedado, one of Havana's most elegant neighborhoods.

Alberto's fortunes had notably declined. In America, his wife was the factory owner, the breadwinner, who begrudgingly gave him an allowance that barely covered his bar tab. She supported him and her extended family by manufacturing girdles just outside of Hialeah. Victoria's daughter, Estersita, was also among the recipients of her charity. Apparently, so was I, now that I was fatherless.

Cousin Alberto pointed the Lincoln toward the dull neon of Estersita's Miami Beach neighborhood. We pulled up to her low, white-bricked apartment building on Pennsylvania Avenue, where she had booked us for an indefinite stay at the Royal Hotel across the street. There was nothing royal about it. Alberto stared as a woman with creased, tanned skin and a halter top several sizes too small worked herself into a furious private dance in front of the hotel's entrance. My sister and brother cried from exhaustion and the strangeness of the new place. "*Por Dios*," Victoria muttered. I didn't know whom among us annoyed her most.

Estersita lived on the ground floor of the apartment building in just four rooms with her husband, Pepé, and their three children: Rosie, León, and Rudolfó. Rosie was, like me, the oldest, but a few years meaner. From the moment I left Alberto's car, Rosie had her eye on my Barbie and the black patent-leather Barbie wardrobe that I carried like a small suitcase. Looking around the room she shared with her brothers, I missed the spaciousness of 1735 Asylum Avenue. The box fan sitting in the midst of what was both living room and dining room broke up the humidity. John, who was now notably less bereft than Carol or I, immediately discovered that talking into the fan distorted his voice, a novelty that delighted him for hours.

It was dusk when we finally walked over to the Royal Hotel. In hindsight, I suspected that my mother was purposely delaying the moment of stepping over the threshold of the dilapidated two-story building. A number of the hotel's elderly residents were parked beneath the sun-faded dark green awning, many of them in wheelchairs or in front of their walkers. They formed a kind of sleepy honor guard as we dragged our suitcases into a lobby that was warmer than Estersita's apartment. An episode of *The Beverly Hillbillies* blared from the lobby's black-and-white television. The woman behind the desk introduced herself as the owner; my mother called her *la dueña*. She wore her gray frizzy hair in a tight ponytail, making the mole on her upper lip all the more prominent. She was an Americana who complained that there were too many Cubans in Miami. She showed us up to our room and took her time pointing out the hot plate, the clothesline, and the two double beds for the four of us.

"We need more space," the Duchess of 1735 Asylum told la dueña.

"This is what your cousin booked for you."

"I don't live like this in Connecticut," my mother said.

"Maybe you should go back."

She knew from the looks of us that we couldn't go back. Not nearly enough time had passed for my father to plead with us to return to Connecticut. Or maybe we would never go home. It was not hard for someone to sense that my mother was on her own with the three children she called her *cola*—her tail, where she was at the head and we fanned out behind her, though never quite forming the orderly line into which she had hoped we'd fall.

"This is what your father has done to us," my mother announced as soon as la dueña left us to settle into the room, where the screen windows had convenient holes for vampire mosquitos to suck our blood. Did my father know that Estersita had reserved a world of poverty for us? Would he rescue us from the not-so-Royal Hotel?

The first morning in our room, my mother scrubbed my urine-soaked sheets in the tub and hung them on the clothesline outside our windows. They were like a semaphore code for Estersita and Rosie to know we were up and about, and they came around looking for a breakfast invitation. It didn't take Rosie long to figure out that someone had wet the bed. It took no time for Carol, who fled the bed she shared with me, to give me up.

"Baby, baby," Rosie taunted me. She had on a mood ring and said it would turn as yellow as my urine if I wore it. Yellow, a scared baby. "Here, put it on," she said, shoving the ring onto my middle finger, but instead of turning yellow, the stone stayed as black as the grime on the hot plate.

After the first week, there was still no word from my father. No glittery Valentine's Day-like cards from him in the Royal Hotel mail; maybe he had run out of stamps. No phone calls from him on the communal telephone; perhaps he didn't know the number. He seemed to have disappeared.

I could wait no longer and took matters into my hands, trying to dial him from Estersita's apartment while she manicured her neighbor's nails. It was a hazy afternoon. The jumpy television broadcast a *novelita* in loud rainbow colors that my mother watched half-heartedly. We were acclimating to spending the summer days indoors while my nonswimming mother worked up the courage to take us to the beach.

I had never made a long-distance call. After a number of false starts, I dialed the operator for help. She asked if I had my parents' permission to place a call to Connecticut.

"I don't need permission to call my father," I told the operator.

"Oh yes you do, honey," said the woman. "Where's your mother?"
I panicked and hung up.

A few minutes later the telephone rang and I heard Estersita yell into the receiver trying to say Connecticut, but it came out as "Coh netee coot," the same way my abuelos pronounced it.

"*Ay chica*," Estersita lectured me, "*una llamada a Coh netee Coot se cuesta*." A phone call spanning the Eastern Seaboard was expensive. *Se cuesta* is a reflexive verb in Spanish; in translation it can imply that the call made itself, that the call had its own physical properties. One small change to *me cuesta* and the phrase meant "it costs me."

Everything in Miami cost me. If I longed to hear my father's voice, *me cuesta*. It cost me that he had gone as absent as a black starless sky.

I asked la dueña every day if I had any mail. If I couldn't be with my father, at least I wanted to see his perfect, primary-school print in rainbow colors on an envelope, with my name in blue ink on the front, his on the return address in green, and for good measure, the address once again on the envelope flap in red ink. I wanted my father's Valentine's Day card in July.

"Nothing," said la dueña sharply. "*Nada para Señorita Judith Frances Bolton.*"

My Bolton grandparents wrote, however. They sent money with the intention of moving us to a hotel with air conditioning, to a place where Mom's bathing suit with the pretty gold buttons would not disappear from the clothesline. Instead of moving us out of the Royal Hotel, my mother used the money to play the role of the rich Americano's wife. She treated Estersita and family to breakfasts at the Cuban diner. We'd kick off the day with *café con leche* and toasted *pan Cubano*, slathered with butter the way my mother drenched us in tanning lotion against the strong Miami sun.

I existed on *batidos de mamey*—the tropical fruit shake my mother said she had been craving ever since she was pregnant with Carol. I loved to moustache my lip with the frothy orange-colored milkshake. Looking back, the shake marked the beginning of my love of all things Cubano and Spanish. I was my father's daughter in that way.

I loved being able to order in Spanish. My accent was getting better, it masked my poor vocabulary, and with each passing day I learned a new word and put sentences together.

I had been more bilingual back when I was a toddler who spoke only Spanish to my mother and my abuelos. "*No Engleesh*," my abuelo told strangers at the drugstore where he bought me M&M's. "*Veinte-cinco centavos*," I translated for him efficiently. "*Ella habla Spaneesh perfectamente*," he proudly told the cashier. For a time, I had glided through the language without translating from English to Spanish in my head.

The Spanish I came to speak in Miami Beach rested somewhere between my mother's rapid-fire fluency and the drawn-out *a*'s and *e*'s of Dad's stilted Americano Spanish, the relic of his bachelor days traveling through Central America. I moved beyond my imposter syndrome—the girl with the good accent without the words to carry on a conversation—and slipped deeper into Spanish. *Pan Cubano y un café con leche*, I finally said in a single breath at the diner. Although I was still the *Americanita*, I finally spoke *español sin un accento*. "*Mira que esta Americanita ahora habla Español muy bien*," my Miami relatives complimented me.

I could feel myself going from American to Cuban. From Hartford to Miami Beach. From Bolton to Alboukrek. From a wet bed to a dry one. From two parents to one.

I tried to call my father again from Estersita's. This time I figured out how to dial directly, but there was no answer. "Daddy isn't home," I whispered to Carol.

"Try again," she said with an edge of panic in her voice.

I dialed again, deliberately placing my finger in each hole of the rotary dial, skeptical that I was registering the correct numbers. "Maybe the phone doesn't work," I said.

I dialed slowly, so that it was less likely someone would hear me. The line clicked its way to West Hartford and I pictured the white phone on the kitchen wall ringing. I hoped my father would answer. Instead, I concluded that each ring faded out in the empty house. Where in the world was he? Was he in one of those places I saw when I watched the panel show *What in the World?*

Matilde with Judy, Carol, and John at a 1970 family wedding in Miami.

Sneaking another call became too risky; eventually I stopped trying
to get a line to Connecticut. My father was never coming for us. I would
be like the lonely child protagonists I voraciously read about in novels I
ordered from the Scholastic Book Club. I prepared myself for life as a
latchkey kid—a life with a volatile mother as my only parent.

Carol and I slunk onto the couch and turned on the television. We
adjusted the rabbit ears to catch a telenovela. We didn't always understand what they were saying, but we could relate to the exaggerated
emotions.

Later that night, the living room was crowded with expat Cubanos trying to listen to Fidel Castro. Pepé, Estersita's husband, adjusted the rabbit ears until the electronic snow gave way to a fuzzy picture of Castro—*el lider, el maximo*—with his wooly, raggedy beard, a beard that was an affront to the smooth-shaven men in Langley, Virginia, and in Washington, DC and the Cubanos in Miami.

Watching *el lider maximo* in Havana, in his drab military uniform with a lidded cap, made me feel farther away from my father. Castro spoke in one long, highly animated streak of breath like the other Cubans I knew in Miami. Pepé and his poker buddies screamed, "*Hijo de mala madre*" at the screen. The ladies at Estersita's manicure table joined the men in cursing Castro's jerky, scrolling television image. These were Cubans stranded just ninety miles from Havana, desperate to tune in Castro every time the wind brought his gray profile into their living rooms.

On that night, the CIA had not spiked Castro's coffee with LSD or poisoned his rum. His cigar did not explode. CIA agents did not get close enough to dust *el lider*'s shoes with thallium salts to make his hair and beard fall out, when he might lose his strength as Samson did after Delilah cut off his hair. None of these rumored fears came to pass for the evening. For the time being, *el lider maximo* would not lose his machismo. And to prove his sobriety, he jabbed an index finger in the air and spoke in a pellucid Spanish that came to us all the way from La Plaza de la Revolución.

Yet his voice sounded hoarse from broadcasting interference. Estersita's neighbors continuously drifted in and out of the apartment, trailing behind them whispers of, "*Cuba, Cuba. Mi Cuba adorada.*" But Castro was indifferent to Cuban suffering in the diaspora. La Plaza del la Revolución could have been on the silvery moon just as well as in tarnished Havana. In the end, Castro's resilience was as maddening to my relatives as it was to the CIA. "No one can get rid of this bastard," I had heard my father say at one of my parents' parties.

I took in the crowded scene of anxious Cubans through the rose-tinted sunglasses I had swiped in a fit of pique at the Rexall. I gripped the small red pocketbook I had never returned to one of the Nancy's in school—puckered and pouched—that I closed with a braided black string. I knew Rosie had her eye on my adorable purse, too, just as I had had my eye on my classmates' possessions.

I got up for more ice cream. Just when I passed the television, the room burst into exclamation. *"Para!"* One of the poker players screamed for me to stop. *"No te muevas!"*

I had stumbled upon the sweet spot in the room where the reception was perfect, as long as I kept standing there.

The room was abuzz. *"Mira eso. La Americanita regló la televisión."* I had fixed the television.

"Por Dios, Castro talks forever. *La niña* can't stand there all night," my mother said.

"She can for ten cents an hour," Pepé bellowed.

Night after night I became a human antenna, collecting dimes and saving them in my little red purse. If I loaded enough change into a pay-phone, perhaps I would finally connect with my father over a thousand miles away in Connecticut. I wanted to go home, to go back north where it was cooler. North, where my parents were still in love.

The telegram arrived six weeks into our muggy stay at the Royal Hotel: Dad was finally coming to rescue us, but for me the gesture was too little and too late. A week before he joined us, he sent his Fort Lauderdale cousins to move us into a hotel on upper Collins Avenue. I had never met these relatives, although they were bit players in Dad's stories about growing up in New Haven. Cousin Bernice and her two sisters had spent their childhood summers on the Connecticut shore with Dad and Aunt Gladys. They were Grandpa's nieces—the daughters of his adored sister Dora, who played the piano during silent movies in New Haven's theaters. Bernice's husband, Bob, was a pharmacist. They were kinder and more even-keeled than Estersita and Pepé.

"If I were sick," I said to Cousin Bob, "you could give me medicine."

"I hope you're never sick," said Bob, the most genial relative I had ever met. "I've got a soda fountain in my drugstore. Maybe you'll get discovered there like Lana Turner."

I didn't know who Lana Turner was, but I liked the idea of someone finding me, paying attention to me. Cousin Bob was sweet when I asked if his soda fountain served batidos de mamey. "I don't know what that is," he said, "but I'm sure we can figure it out."

"She wets the bed," Carol said, butting into the conversation and upending my fantasy of spinning on stools while sipping a milkshake at Cousin Bob's pharmacy.

Bernice and Bob drove us up Collins Avenue past stretches of white sand beaches, past the Fontainebleau hotel, and all the way up to motel row, where we decamped to the Colonial Inn. The moment I walked into the cool, orderly lobby, I knew that my father's pending arrival was the only reason we were moving into more comfortable circumstances. For him, there was a private color television so that he could watch *Upstairs, Downstairs* on Masterpiece Theater. There was air conditioning and activities for children so that my parents could reunite. We drew pictures and painted plaster figures in the basement playroom, all for his convenience.

I was painting the headdress of an Indian chief in peacock colors when I spied my mother running up to my father and clinging to him. She was crying. My father, calm and collected, walked into the playroom. Tanned and trim, he carried a battered monogrammed valise, splattered with the rain that kept us indoors that day. Carol and John ran into his arms. He was wearing the same billowy khakis I had seen in his vacation pictures from Guatemala.

I turned my attention back to the square-chinned Indian chief.

With Carol and John in each arm, Dad came up to me. "A hug for your dad?" he asked. I continued painting, muddying the colors of the chief's headdress, remembering the phone calls he hadn't answered. "You've always been your mother's girl," he said. He put down Carol and John and walked out of the room.

"You're mean," my sister said, stamping her foot.

John, who repeated everything Carol said, added, "Daddy won't ever take you to the pool with us."

That made no difference to me. I didn't know how to swim. My father had not followed the Talmudic dictum to teach one's child to survive in the water.

My father was back and just as mysterious as he had ever been. He never told us what he had done during all that time without us, or where he had been that he couldn't answer the kitchen phone.

CHAPTER 12

The Clairvoyant Trifecta

While the Bolton side of the family breathed in the rarefied air of New Haven in a state the Alboukreks of Havana could not pronounce, the Latino side of my family has always been in conversation with the dead. Grandma Bolton showered me with *pooh, pooh*'s and *kinah hora*'s as she exhorted various whip-tailed spirits to stay away from my crib, but the Latinos had their own brand of magic and mystery. They are a people who open doors cautiously, expecting at any moment to come upon a random spirit.

My abuela consulted about malevolent spirits with her God—*El Dio de la zedakades*, a singular charitable God. Not the plural-sounding "Dios" for the rest of the Latinos. Sephardic Jews understood, perhaps better than their Ashkenazi counterparts, that "The Lord is God, The Lord is one."

Abuela whispered to me in Ladino, "*Que Dio la guarda.*" May God keep her. In the middle of the night she wiped my face with my urine-soaked diapers to keep jealous spirits away. She had done the same for her children to guard their health and to coax forth the beauty of her daughters.

In me, a single baby united by two disparate cultures, each faction desired to exert their influence. One grandmother soothed me in Spanish and Ladino. The other worried I would not be able to communicate with her in English. No one at the time was aware that a bilingual brain stretches to accommodate other languages, or that a bilingual baby can accommodate many cultures.

My grandmothers thought they were giving me the divergent blessings of their ancestors, but they were closer to each other in spirit and intent than they realized. "Don't tell your father," my mother said the first time she took me to see a medium. I saw her point. And yet my father's mother spat into cribs to ward off evil spirits.

Jews are not supposed to consult with mediums, but in my mother's universe, acquiring a husband was the truest faith, and the first time she went to Margaríta it was to consult about her marriage. "*Tiene que ser un mujeriego,*" my mother complained during the readings where I sat quietly in the background, but Margaríta assured her that Harold was not a ladies' man, while agreeing with solemnity that "he had his *secreticos.*"

My mother transplanted her tropical Cuba to my father's freezing Connecticut with her visits to Margaríta, a Cubana, a woman my mother called *mi negra*, my Black one. Margaríta knew things. Brown and rotund, with a short blonde wig that sat askew on her head, Margaríta read *las cartas*, the tarot cards. My mother took me to her when I was a child to inquire about our family's health and her children's fates. All Margaríta ever demanded in payment were two packages of Oscar Meyer Pickle & Pimento Loaf and a large bottle of Sprite, which we purchased at Arthur's Drugstore one door down from her apartment building.

In my early twenties, when I was convinced that I was dying of a broken heart, my mother took me on a return trip to Margaríta. She was convinced that the ghost of my abuela could help bring my boyfriend Michael back to me.

"Your abuela is *cerquita, cerquita,*" close by, Margaríta confirmed.

I was sixteen to Michael's eighteen when I first met him by way of my abuela and Michael's ancient, stony great-grandfather, whose rooms were across the hall from each other at the Hebrew Home. Abuela was only in her early seventies but had been immobile in one way or another for as long as I could remember, surrounded by light brown pill bottles to treat everything from hypertension to diabetes. No one could pin down exactly what was wrong with her, but she traced her problems back to her difficult delivery when my mother arrived a month early, twelve pounds at birth. The doctor told my abuela that another pregnancy was too dangerous, yet my Aunt Reina arrived fourteen months later—and Uncle José seven years after that, despite Abuela's attempts to miscarry by softening her cervix with olive oil and taking scalding baths.

After her husband died, Abuela refused to walk again. Even so, sending her to the Hebrew Home was heresy for a Sephardic family that worshipped our imperious matriarchs as much as we worshipped an enigmatic God. Abuela spent her final days in a wheelchair muttering prayers to the God of her ancestors to let her die.

But before Abuela died, there was a match to be made between me and Michael, the great-grandson of the centenarian across the hall. That first blind date was set in motion when my mother, during a visit to her mother, glimpsed Michael's rosy-cheeked and white-toothed high school graduation portrait his grandmother had presented for inspection. I was a year behind Michael in school and my graduation photos were still in proofs—dark circles under my eyes, acne spattered across my forehead, but he called anyway. No boy had ever called me.

Michael was the most grown-up teenager I had ever seen. Rugby-shirted and tall, with dark curly hair, he came to pick me up in his mother's beige Dodge Dart. When I answered the door, he looked past me. "I'm here for your sister," he said, mistaking me for a child.

Despite his misgivings, we went on a date that lasted eight years.

Michael left for his freshman year of college a couple of weeks after we made out on the sofa in his den. His house was big and square and cluttered with dark, menacing antiques. No one was allowed to sit on the brocaded sofas in the living room, so Michael climbed on top of me in his den, unbuttoning my shirt. Suddenly his mouth was on my small breasts. I thought he was rearranging my heart. I thought, this is what loves feels like.

Michael was the new mystery in my life. My passion for him knew no limits. Or did it? My anxiety over being the perfect girlfriend did not focus exclusively on sex, but on pleasing him in some nobler, more spiritual way. Only in hindsight did I realize how the mystery of Michael was just the mystery of my father, once removed. If I couldn't solve the one, perhaps I'd have more luck with the other.

In my junior year of college, while my classmates went to Rome or Paris or London, I went to Michael. I babysat him in Baltimore while he applied to medical schools. Although I took a full complement of English literature classes while I was at Johns Hopkins, it was as if I were majoring in Michael.

Then the panic attacks started.

Panic wasn't new to the women of my family. "Commit me, commit me," my mother said throughout my childhood, often gulping air. And then this: "*Estoy tan cansada.*" I am so exhausted.

"My mother was a sick woman, in and out of hospitals," my mother always said. Sick with what, she never elucidated, while Grandma Bolton never fully recuperated from her postpartum depression and once told me she avoided my grandfather, sleeping in another bedroom by her mid-thirties.

Would I inherit my grandmother's anxiety about sex? When I was fourteen, I hid the curves of my body beneath baggy, long-sleeved shirts, and skirts that fell well below the knee. I imagined that my future groom would be a learned Jewish man with a long, scraggly beard. In private he'd radiate the color of the sun. He'd thrill to hold my hand when permitted. Our sex, though rule-bound, would be romantic.

"You learn what pleases a man," the woman in charge of teaching the laws of family purity at the Yeshiva let slip.

As time went on, between Michael's philandering and my mother's unreasonable expectations for maintaining my virginity, I lived the double life of a good girl who sometimes thought she did bad things.

"Men need women," my mother declared. Yet, to her, those women were not the kind a man married. I had grown up with Mom's clarion call never to let a man touch me below the neck. She had a laundry list of courtship rules by which to live by, perhaps made clearer to her after tutoring the unwed mothers at Saint Agnes Home:

If a man touches your *tetas,* you will lose control and then lose every-
   thing.
Touch your cookie only to clean it. Do not clean it for too long.
Never talk to a man with a tattoo.
Marry a Jewish boy.
Marry a professional Jewish boy.
If you use tampons, you will lose your virginity.
If you wash your hair on the first day of your period, you will be infer-
   tile.
Do not paint your toenails red. Only *chusma* girls have red toenails.
Chusma girls wear ankle bracelets and snap gum.
High heels make your legs prettier.
No sneakers.
Wear slippers with a heel at home. Your husband will like that.
Grow your hair long. Brush it a lot so you don't have *bolones*—knots.
Wax your eyebrows every two weeks.
Swing your *culo* slightly when you walk so that you are appealing yet
   still a lady.

My mother's rules had done little to prepare me for dating. Religious
strictures that I had learned at the yeshiva only made life more confusing.
During my time there, I thought I'd be obligated to purify myself monthly
in a *mikveh,* a ritual bath, before resuming sexual relations with my future
husband. For two weeks per month of *tumah,* I'd be forbidden to touch
him, look into his eyes, or even hand anything to him directly. It was only
permissible to be naked in front of one's husband under the blackest
night sky or in the darkest of rooms.

Whatever my conflicts were over sex, God, and my mother's ruling
hand, one thing was certain to me: No one had ever loved a man more
than I loved Michael. No one was willing to sacrifice as much as I did for
him.

If Margaríta the medium divined that I was already sleeping with
Michael, she had the presence of mind to not share it with my mother.
She studied the oversized tarot cards that displayed men in robes, knights

on horses, damsels in distress. From this array of images she discerned that a blonde woman was keeping me apart from my beloved. "*La madre!*" shouted my mother. Michael's mother never liked our Latina ways and, according to my mother's interpretation of the medium's message, had engineered the breakup.

Wrapping up, Margaríta had good news for me: Her cards showed another man in my future. "His name has three letters," she reported. "He is a good man. He is fair and blue-eyed."

She ended the session with some low-key pyrotechnics. From one of myriad candles burning in the middle of the afternoon in her dark, three-room apartment, she lit a thick, half-smoked cigar and, to my alarm, put the burning end of it in her mouth. Smoke billowed from her ears. After she stubbed out the cigar she gave me instructions: "Bathe in water and honey and pray to Santá Aná," patron saint of the lovelorn.

My mother sat quietly during these somber instructions.

Once again, all Margaríta asked for in return was some Oscar Meyer Pickle & Pimento Loaf and a bottle of Sprite.

"Remember, don't tell your father," my mother cautioned. "The bath won't work, the cards won't mean anything if you tell."

Decades later, and happily married to a fair and blue-eyed man with three letters that made up his name, Ken, I was back to figuring out the essential mystery in my life: my father. I paid a visit to Josh.

Josh had an unlikely profile for a medium. He was in his early forties and handsome—black curly hair, steady ocean-blue eyes, and a how-ya-doin' demeanor. He was a member of my temple, a nice Jewish boy, the kind of boy a Jewish mother loves.

But Josh had had a near-death experience, and that changed everything for him. There had been no white light or underground tunnel, just a gentle message from his grandfather telling him that it was not Josh's time yet. "Go back to your family," the old man instructed. And so Josh returned to this life with the power to communicate with the dead. He pierced our rabbi's skepticism when he correctly described the rabbi's father, who had been dead for three decades. Josh's vision of the dead man's eyeglasses tucked away in his wife's nightstand was eerily accurate.

He continued to be precise and correct in front of the small temple audience, bringing messages from departed loved ones.

In the rabbi's introduction to Josh's synagogue session, he cautioned that fortune-telling was one of the more non-Jewish activities in which the congregation might indulge. And yet he may have been as intrigued as Saul was when, against his own legislation "forbidding recourse to ghosts and familiar spirits in the land," Saul consulted with the Witch of Endor to conjure the dead prophet Samuel. Saul was frightened of the Philistines and asked Samuel if he would survive their impending attack. Samuel, annoyed at being called back into this world, predicted Saul's death.

I saw Josh in his home for a private consultation with my dead. As soon as he opened the door he affably said, "I've been meditating this morning in preparation for our meeting. Do the letters *K* or *H* mean anything to you?"

K. Harold Bolton. Yes, those letters meant something to me. But that was an easy one—possibly a Google find.

We were standing in Josh's living room amid Christmas stockings, a menorah, and a shrine to Buddha. I was more astonished by this bevy of cultural and religious markers than I was that Josh had intuited my father's initials.

"One thing I learned when I almost died is that there is no right way to do things," Josh said as he began our session.

I asked him if he believed in God. "How can I not?" he said. It was the open-ended answer of a man who had been to the other side and come back to apply here what he learned there.

He concentrated for a moment. "I see an old woman, a grandmother maybe, sitting next to you," he said. "I'm getting a strong vision of the letter *A*."

Grandma Anna Bolton, the Anna for whom my daughter was named. Grandma was not Googleable. Neither was my daughter.

Grandma and I have a phantasmagoric relationship. Her ghost came to me when I was first married. I was alone, dressing for a friend's wedding. My grandmother loved seeing me dressed up; when I was a little girl she bought me clothing from the Edward Malley Company in New Haven. "A little model girl," she said when I tried on the outfits. "A *shayna punim*," she said taking my face in her hands. "Beautiful."

"She's a sort of guardian angel for you," said Josh.

I burst into tears.

I was not the first person to come looking for the dead in Josh's living room, and he was prepared. There was a box of Kleenex on the coffee table. He assumed the gentle, supportive stance of medium-cum-therapist.

In my second session with Josh, Grandma Bolton was still by my side. Whereas with Margaríta the future mingled with everyday details of the present, Josh breathed deeply and sighed his way into my past. This time, he said he saw my father pass by, and I thought of the way the moon passed over the sun to temporarily blacken the world—the eclipse for which he had so carefully prepared the family.

"He's not saying much," Josh said. "He's telling me to look up Guatemala on a map. Do you know why he would say that?"

I hadn't told Josh about Dad's time in Guatemala. Nor had I mentioned Ana. He said Dad was whispering to him about a woman named Ana from Guatemala.

"Ana is his daughter. He's holding up four fingers," Josh said solemnly.

A finger for each of his children! My dead father was acknowledging me, confirming my suspicions, a redemption of sorts. I wasn't crazy after all.

I connected Dad's four children to a version of the four children of the Haggadah—the wise, the wicked, the simple, and the child who simply does not know. I was the girl detective. I was the child who wanted to know.

A year later I handed five crisp hundred-dollar bills to Sarah, another medium, to see if she could unveil more of my parents' mysteries. Sarah was in the business of "getting the right people on line." Listening afterward to the scratchy tape of our session, the transaction sounded illicit. I told Sarah that I had so many questions about my father. Why was he in Latin America? Who was Ana, really? I must have sounded desperate.

I had paid for a fifty-minute hour, and for this abridged hour we were in a room in a Marriott Courtyard in West Hartford. Sarah, who was in her late fifties, had short blonde hair, nondescript clothing, and was barefoot. She began by observing that my father was the first spirit to show up for our session. She definitely had him "on the line," she said.

Throughout our session, Sarah was keen to establish her credentials. She correctly identified the months in which family birthdays and anniversaries occurred. She presented a veritable alphabet of initials for me, all of them creepily applicable to important names in my life. As she went through these personal statistics, it occurred to me that if she were an enterprising sort she might have gleaned all this information from the Internet, where by then I was regularly blogging about my life. But her next question astonished me.

"Who got Dad's watch?" Sarah asked. I felt myself blanch. I had never written publicly about my father's watch, nor had I thought about it in years. The watch had disappeared in the ashes of my brother's difficult divorce. To this day I mourn its loss. My father's watch always stood out. Sturdy, elegant, dependable like him, the watch—a college graduation gift from Grandma and Grandpa Bolton in 1940—was a talisman from another world. It was a silent witness to his five years in the Navy during the Second World War. It was on his wrist throughout his travels in Latin America.

Sarah told me that Dad confirmed he had four children. Just when I was getting excited, she abruptly announced that my father wanted me to "let sleeping dogs lie, because if you knew the specifics it might cause some stir-ups." Sarah had nothing else that sounded credible to tell.

After I left Sarah's hotel room, I was still astonished about the watch. I called a friend to burble about it. She sighed deeply. "These so-called mediums use that watch question all the time," she said. "Think about it: Most dads of your father's generation have a special watch. It's a safe question for a charlatan to use."

Deflated, I made a pact with myself not to ask any more strangers to disturb my dead. The dead would come to me in due course.

CHAPTER 13

Silent Symphony

Grandpa Bolton died on a bone-cold day in January of 1980, and my father cried for his father, the model immigrant, the hero of family lore. He cried for his father's guidance, for the letters that walked him through creating a household budget. He cried for the sentimental poems Grandpa penned that declared his love of family or that celebrated Yale touchdowns. He cried that Grandpa's topcoat was too small for him or my brother, but fit me perfectly. He cried because he would never eat Grandpa's *matzoh brei* again.

He cried because he was no longer anyone's son.

When my father retreated into his small, spartan closet to drink, I knew, even when I was nineeen, that he took with him precious memories of life with his parents—memories as bright to him as the light of day. His quiet, tamped-down behavior was in contrast to the aggressive drinker mode I knew when I was younger. One cold night, when we were all embattled in the house, he drunk-drove us to the mall, and a terrified woman jumped out of his way as he hit the curb. Another time, he frightened a gaggle of my friends as he drove us home, inebriated, from a bar mitzvah.

Sometimes he was a silly drunk. "POTS," he yelled, saying the word STOP backwards as he ran a stop sign. He wiggled his fingers as if communicating in some crazy sign language.

After I grew up, Dad's life was still as circumscribed and cramped as that closet. During football season he took his transistor radio, tuned to

WELI, into that tight space. It became his habit to sit on the floor amid the golf shoes he no longer wore, the cabana shirts, along with the moth-eaten jackets my grandmother had once picked out for him at J. Press. The bottle of vodka under the kitchen sink migrated with him to that closet. He sat in a coffin-like darkness and drank until he passed out. My father was tired. He was sixty plus years old and his memories over-whelmed him.

After my father's death, discovering the essence of K. Harold Bolton became more urgent for me. Cleaning out his closet, I thought I had that chance when I stumbled upon his own father's unpublished autobiogra-phy, simply titled "My Memoirs." It felt like the find of the century, a sunken treasure chest. I cleared away my father's shoe trees and dug out the manuscript, carefully handling the yellowing legal-size loose-leaf sheets. There within that book would be the truth, unbidden and rare. A truth that might finally reveal some of the mysteries my father had kept to himself, and that I felt were my birthright to know. I sat on the floor of the closet with the manuscript the way my father had sat there with his bottle of Stoli.

Grandpa began his life story slowly, with sections on his fondness for making apple cider, harvesting ice, and growing up in the Connecticut countryside. There was Grandpa driving his father's horse and wagon, delivering milk, or fetching firewood. That memory led him to muse about the wonders of modern refrigeration, electricity, and the introduc-tion of the first car. These entries were quaint but began to frustrate me. The book was blurry in its recall, trivial in subject. Where was Grandpa in these pages? Where was my father?

I remembered Grandpa writing and rewriting his book when I was a child, and now I saw that with each pass he must have sanitized his per-sonal history until there were only a few scattered sentences that even mentioned his children or grandchildren. There were passages about the mayor of New Haven who made him retire at seventy, and about Grand-pa's engineering colleagues, and most certainly about the friends he made in the music business.

He gave my father's birth a single sentence.

The glare of Grandpa's sparkling story of himself as a successful young immigrant, a graduate of no less than Yale, blinded him—and me—to a deeper story that would illuminate secrets and solve mysteries. That he was a Jew hardly deserved a mention in the book of his life. This was the heritage Grandpa passed down to my father, who prized being an American above any other identity. Grandpa imparted so little personal information that the reader ends up learning more about the city of New Haven's murky sewer system, which he dealt with as a civil engineer, than Grandpa's interior life. He never says explicitly that he was born in Ukraine in 1891. There is virtually no history around his family's immigration except for the curious fact that his father immigrated twice. He never says that the family's original, pre-Anglicized name was Bolotin.

As I pored over those pages, increasingly crestfallen, I saw that my grandfather had devoted merely a page to falling in love with my grandmother, "a buxom, lithe, gorgeous creature." He reported that when he walked Grandma home from his prom at Yale, where he had spent the evening playing his violin in the orchestra pit, both of them hummed "I'm Falling in Love with Someone" from Victor Herbert's *Naughty Marietta*.

"The song," Grandpa wrote, "was a significant theme throughout my sixty-four years of married life, and incidentally my favorite violin solo."

Rather than include glossy photographs of his children and grandchildren, Grandpa's memoir featured blueprints for the sewage plants he had designed. For much of my father's life, his own father—engineer, musician, poet, the man who willed himself into the American dream—eclipsed him.

What I gleaned from myriad readings of Grandpa's book is that the gentle grandfather I knew, the man who became a successful orchestra leader and had a lucrative day job as a civil engineer, was also a man whose ambition took root in his sepia-tinged boyhood on a farm in Branford, Connecticut. Grandpa wrote that he began his days at four-thirty in the morning to feed the cattle, the chickens, and the horses. Twelve hours later, after he had been to school, he practiced his violin for an hour. His family cut the household budget razor-thin to give their standout son music lessons. When Willy touched bow to string, his parents knew that their boy had talent. And though they might not have understood it that way at the time, my great-grandparents must have sensed that Grandpa's musical ability, coupled with America's social mobility, would enable him to move ahead in life at dizzying speed.

Grandpa played his first professional gig at fourteen at a tony country club on Long Island as part of a quartet. He traveled part of the way in a sleigh and was woozy from the cold until someone warmed him up with a hot toddy. It was the first time he was drunk.

He fiddled his way through Yale on union pay to afford tuition and the right clothes in which to go to classes with the likes of Cole Porter. I imagine that Porter played piano in the rarefied company of Yale's sons, while Grandpa played at dances in fraternity houses to which he would otherwise never be admitted. But it was his friend and classmate Jack Cipriano, whose talent at the piano Grandpa described as magnificent, who "played an important role in my life."

Grandpa mentioned his social status at Yale in the briefest of moments when he described an encounter with a professor who refused to excuse him from class the day after playing all night at a Labor Day party. "Poor boys should not attempt to go to college if outside work interferes with their studies," the professor scoffed. Grandpa prevailed, doing what he did best: working his connections in the union and in the dean's office. It turns out the dean's daughter knew Grandpa from the various dances she attended and was a big fan.

As I read on the floor of Dad's closet, I understood that my grandfather's ambition had intimidated my father. Unlike Dad, my grandparents married early—just six months after Grandpa's graduation from Yale in 1913. In my grandfather's work as an engineer, he was careful to cultivate the status and manners that came with being a professional. Although he never said it explicitly, Grandpa was a spectator in a world that did not welcome Jews; yet his book suggested that he wanted things to be different for my dad. All of this came about as he trailblazed his way into the heart of an America where he was both accepted and marginalized.

At the beginning of my own violin studies, my father, whom grandpa taught, frequently practiced with me, hoping I would squeak out a recognizable tune. Practices had the gravity of carrying on a family tradition, something of which even as a child I was aware. It thrilled me to share violin playing with my father, even if I was nowhere close to mastering the instrument. It gave us a shared vocabulary, a common experience.

Our time always began the same way: Dad tucking my quarter-size violin under his chin to tune it for me. As he turned the black wooden pegs—to tighten the nylon strings into the right pitch, a fifth apart, something he did wholly by ear—he was a one-man orchestra tuning up. In a final flourish he perfectly captured the violin's harmony when he played the strings together. As he handed the violin back to me, he regarded the tiny instrument with awe. "I had no idea they made these so little," he said almost every time, positioning my head on the chin rest.

In the six years that I attempted to play the violin, my father asked the same question to a succession of my teachers: "Does she have any talent?" In that time, he was witness to me bowing in the wrong direction, to fingering that fell short of playing in tune, and to my overall musical illiteracy. Many years after he quietly brought my full-size violin to sell back to the music store, I understood that playing the violin for my father was not about achieving perfection; he played because of the love and desire that music stirred in him.

The time my father visited me at my faux-espionage job in Manhattan, we wandered the Upper West Side together looking for records that pleased him, especially light opera and Viennese waltzes. There were also recordings of the music of Spain that Dad had played on his long-ago radio program, zarzuelas and bullfight music. The music had the kind of drama that my father concealed inside himself. We even looked for the music Grandpa had loved—Straus waltzes, the music of Franz Liszt and Victor Herbert. The list was so long and some of the titles were out of print; we couldn't possibly find everything my father wanted that day, but I kept the names of the records he wrote out in green ink on yellow legal-size paper. I combed through more music shops on my own until I found the elusive recording of Herbert's *Naughty Marietta*.

A few years later, I spied my father in the family den shakily conducting Gilbert and Sullivan from his recliner, scratched-up records playing music loudly on the old turntable. By then the Parkinson's had robbed him of most of his voice and his walking—but he was determined and fierce, a king with a scepter, a wizard with a wand, as he pretended that there was an entire orchestra before him to conduct.

I managed to have some musical success with the Suzuki violin method. Learning to play the Suzuki way was like language acquisition. The goal was to listen to the records and follow the music in the practice book, but I found a shortcut and listened intently to the records to imitate the melody, never learning how to read the notes. My father eventually caught on to my musical illiteracy and turned off the hi-fi when I practiced.

Janet Farrar was my last violin teacher. I was a young teenager and her goal was to wean me off the Suzuki method and learn to read music. She came to the house on Saturday mornings in a dark blue Volkswagen that matched the corduroy pants she always wore. Miss Farrar brought her own metronome and a viola instead of a violin. "It's just a slightly larger instrument and has a string an octave lower. The harmony will be exquisite when we play together," she explained cheerfully.

Miss Farrar wanted to be Annie Sullivan to my Helen Keller, but I was hopelessly trapped in my unmusical body. In addition to teaching me to read music, Miss Farrar was resolute about correcting my bowing. Each time I bowed in the wrong direction, she gently squeezed my shoulder as opposed to giving me a karate chop like one of my previous teachers had done. When I swayed she put her hand on the small of my back, which stopped me cold with its kind intention. If the piece I was playing was wildly out of tune, she moved my fingers up and down the strings. I desperately wanted to connect to the right fingering to play the music of my father and my grandfather.

Each week Dad lurked outside the living room where I had my lessons as if it were a hospital room he was afraid to enter. Occasionally he'd catch Miss Farrar on her way out and ask her his stock question about my untapped talent. "Listen to all kinds of music with her," she prescribed.

With that, Miss Farrar and her gigantic viola headed back into her small blue bug of a car.

"Let's try something different," said Miss Farrar during one of our final lessons. "Music without playing an instrument."

She introduced me to John Cage's silent symphony, *4′33″*, so named for the four minutes and thirty-three seconds that a performer sits in total quiet. To avoid another frustrating lesson, Miss Farrar and I played our own silent symphony. With our instruments perched on our laps, we sat in a quiet studded with the creaky sounds of the house, with my father's inimitable footfalls up and down the stairs and the cars traveling up and down Asylum Avenue.

My father had hoped I would be a third-generation violinist. There was agency on my part in choosing the violin: I wanted to have something meaningful in common with my father and grandfather. The problem was that I lacked Grandpa's skill or Dad's passion to make music. Each time my father put bow to string, I saw how he closed his eyes and played his way through a piece with a dreamy, blissful focus. He approached every piece of music seriously and lovingly, whether it was a Strauss waltz or one of the rudimentary ditties he practiced with me. In the end, I couldn't continue to imitate something I didn't feel.

After so much time, it's funny what the body remembers. I am fifty-five years-old; I haven't touched a violin since I was fifteen. I thought of Miss Farrar and her viola and of my father tuning my tiny violin as I tucked my father's full-size one under my chin, the one I found in his closet before we left 1735 Asylum forever, and I automatically fingered Vivaldi's *Concerto in A Minor* on the graceful ebony neck. I did not make any sound; it was just my fingers connecting with the strings. The bow in my right hand hung by my side. I trembled in the musical silence that Miss Farrar once created for me.

A few years before he composed *4′33″*, John Cage visited an anechoic chamber—a space completely devoid of noise—to encounter silence in its purest form. Even in that chamber he managed to hear a sound with distinct highs and lows. It turned out that the high sound was his nervous system at work. The low sound was his blood circulating. The body continuously plays its own music in harmony.

Like John Cage, I've heard similar symphonies within my body, complete with the high and low sounds of the soul and the heart. I've heard them in the flaming red of passion and light green of memory. I heard them when I fell in love with my husband. I heard them when my children were born.

The silent symphony was the rhythm of my baby moving inside of me. It was the inadvertent beat of my father's shaking Parkinsonian hand on my pregnant belly. It was the silence before and after the shovelfuls of dirt that made a thwacking noise against the lid of his coffin. It was the silence between regret and forgiveness.

CHAPTER 14

Mazal

I was dangerously close to thirty and still unmarried when my mother dragged me to another fortune teller. We were in Miami for my youngest cousin's bat mitzvah. This time the clairvoyant was Consuelo, who did not live up to her name, which means consolation. She read my misfortune in a dusty beauty parlor where cats draped themselves on the helmeted hair dryers. She had high hopes for my sister, Carol, but said that I would never marry. "You have no mazal," no luck, my mother yelled at me afterward, as if my bad fortune with men were my cosmic fault.

Mazal has always carried a double meaning for me. Mazal Tov is my mother's Hebrew name. In the parlance of traditional Jewish life this made me Yehudit, the daughter of Mazal Tov—the daughter of luck—random, volatile luck. Mazal Tov is a common name for women among my mother's Sephardic clan, but it jolts an Ashkenazic congregation, unaccustomed to hearing Mazal Tov as a name. To this day, when I am called by my Hebrew name to bless the Torah, the Mazal Tov part of my moniker stands out as a verbal comet tail for the congregation, sparkling against a wide, empty sky and lingering for a moment before it fizzles.

My mother, though, was convinced that, because she'd been named after a dead woman in defiance of her family's tradition of naming after the living, her Hebrew name reversed the intended effect of Mazal Tov.

For a time, it seemed that she had handed down her bad luck to me.

Within a few months of Consuelo's gloomy prediction, I met Ken. The first time I mentioned him to my parents, I allowed my mother to exhaust herself on her favorite topic: how unreasonably fussy I was about men. How I might be a lesbian.

"At your age, it's not healthy for you to be without a man," she said.

"Here we go again," my father muttered.

I let their remarks float among us as we sat in the dining room eating Mom's desiccated chicken and overly boiled rice.

"I recently met the man I'm going to marry," I finally said. I let my proclamation wash over them.

Ken and I had met two weeks earlier at his brother Steven's birthday party. I worked with Steven's wife at the Jewish civil rights organization, and she had promised me there would be plenty of single lawyers from his firm—all I had to do was choose one. I was twenty-nine years old and quickly calculated that I was just past the point where I could have a baby before thirty. I had nothing to lose.

As soon as I walked into the room, I made a beeline for the rocking chair, not the lawyers. I was at the party alone and needed to have a way to self-soothe. Next to me was Ken—nameless at first, identifying himself only as Steven's brother. He said little else for the rest of the evening, but the rocking motion calmed me as I took in the rest of the party and I decided to stay where I was. By the time I had had enough of smiling the aching smile of the stranger, Ken and I barely said good-bye. I was surprised when his sister-in-law told me that he wanted to call me.

I didn't have a type, but I mused over how I would not have been inspired by a guy like Ken when I was younger. I had fallen into the Michael trap—tall, dark, and mean—and the Dan trap, another boyfriend, who had been tall, blond, and aloof. Ken was blond and oh so adorable. I gathered he must have been very shy when he didn't have the nerve to ask me out directly. His sister-in-law passed my number along and I didn't hear from him; it turned out she had given him the wrong number. He finally thought to call information after he tried me for several days and got no answer.

When at last he got through, he introduced himself in a soft, gentle voice. I, the hardened, jaded single woman in the city, was smitten. We talked about work, his and mine.

"I have to confess that I have an odd job," I said. "I monitor right-wing extremists."

"Interesting," he said politely. "How do you do that?"

"I read their hate rags, their vile mimeographed newsletters. I'd never seen anything like that until I came to this job."

I was afraid to scare him off by talking about extremists, so I tried to impress him by talking about science instead. His sister-in-law told me he was working on a new venture to map all the genes in the human body.

"I recently read an article about the Human Genome Project," I said, pronouncing genome with a hard *g*. I said it over and over, pleased with my new knowledge.

"I think it's pronounced genome," he finally said with the soft *g*, but he did not laugh at me or tease me. He was patient and more than tolerant of imperfection. In that instant I knew this was the man with the three-lettered name that Margaríta had predicted I was destined to meet.

On our first official date, we took a boat across the Hudson to a place called Arthur's Landing. This was a multipart undertaking that included drinks in New Jersey, dinner on the Upper West Side, and desert near my apartment close to Columbia University. At Arthur's Landing we checked off boxes. We were still young enough to inquire about college majors. We went through our favorite books. I liked that Ken was reading *Moby-Dick*. We said little about previous relationships. However, there was one question I was curious to ask, and a second beer emboldened me: "Have you ever been a sperm donor?"

"No. Why do you ask?"

"Well, you were a poor graduate student for many years. You may have needed the cash."

"I was never that poor. And I like all my children accounted for." He smiled a thin smile, and I couldn't tell if he was amused or incredulous.

"I'm glad you feel that way, because I want to start with a clean slate," I said. "I dated a guy who didn't tell me he had a baby until a couple of months into our relationship. When he invited me to his house for dinner, he warned me I would see something shocking—he shared custody with the baby's mother and had a crib in his apartment. I don't like those kind of surprises."

"I don't blame you," Ken said, taking my hand. "You can rest assured that I have no children anywhere. No baby furniture or diapers in my apartment. Clean slate."

A couple of months later, I brought Ken to Asylum Avenue for the weekend. That "my fellow" was a Princeton graduate thrilled my Ivy League father no end. Although it was hard for me to imagine Dad as anything other than a Yale bulldog, he always said he would have gone to Princeton if not for the Depression. When he entered Yale in the fall of 1936, Dad lived at home to save money. We joked that Dad not only looked like Yale's bulldog mascot; we anthropomorphized that the Malibu looked a bit canine, too.

My wonderful boyfriend listened as my father went on about Dick Kazmaier, Princeton's first and only Heisman Trophy winner. Ken's presence inspired my father to track down Princeton football statistics that had been lurking for decades in the corridors of his brain. Ken was patient. Dad was thrilled.

"Kazmaier wasn't a big guy," Dad reminisced. "Just shy of six feet tall. Played tailback." He trotted out his volume of *The Yale Football Story* to show Ken, the raised blue letters of the title emblazoned on the book's worn gray cover. The book was Dad's *siddur*, his prayer book. It was as close as my father would come to claiming a holy text.

Later, to me, my father took the measure of my guy. "Nice fellow. Refined kid, too. He wasn't born with a silver spoon stuck up his ass like that other one."

Ken came to belong to my father the same way Michael had once belonged to my mother. The first year Michael and I were together, Michael the premed student masqueraded as a Spanish major, and he and my mother read *Don Quijote* together. My mother chirped all over again about Cide Hamete Benengeli—Cervantes's fictional alter ego. With Ken, Dad recalled how the men of Princeton were the truest gentlemen. Michael, the aspiring doctor, reminded my mother of Manuel, the boyfriend she lost long ago. Ken was my father's new buddy—one of the guys Dad loved to trade stories with about his glory days at Yale.

That weekend, each of my parents mortified me in different ways. My father ruffled Ken's hair and asked if he could call him Curly. On Sunday morning when Ken was not in my brother's room, I raced downstairs to find him in the den with my mother—where, like any good publicist, she was pitching me to my boyfriend. They were going through tear sheets of my newspaper articles going back to college. She was also pulling back layers of her family history all the way to the Inquisition. Ken won my mother's fickle heart when he patiently sat for a crash course in Ladino. "In Ladino the *j* sounds like zhhh as in Zsa Zsa Gabor. So, the word for son is pronounced like *hizho*," she said.

"*Hizho*," she said again when Ken and I got engaged six months later.

Mine was the first wedding in the family since Uncle José's. At José's nuptials, my mother rumbled for a fight when she harangued a distant cousin for snubbing her a decade earlier. At my wedding, she set her sights on Dennis, my future father-in-law, who had immersed himself in the wedding preparations. She harrumphed that he was an *abramujer*, a portmanteau word in Ladino and a sharp Sephardic insult that describes a man who asserts himself in traditional women's work.

A friend of my mother's made my unadorned taffeta and raw silk gown, and the only thing I desperately wanted was a bow for the back of the dress. The friend, whom I never saw again after the wedding, was a sour woman who grudgingly made the bow the day before the ceremony. That was the day my mother left me with a bowless gown that still needed to be hemmed with less than thirty-six hours until I walked down the aisle. Mom had had enough of my happiness and said she needed to visit Abuela's grave—yes, that very moment. "I'm going to *el cementerio*," she said over her shoulder as she trotted to a waiting taxi. And then the same threat I had been hearing all my life: "You know, I'll be *seis pies debajo*," six feet below the ground, "sooner than you think."

The morning of my wedding, my mother read circulars from her favorite discount stores. It was an Indian summer day, glorious and bursting with New England color, and she was hunting bargains as if it were the only thing on her schedule.

My wedding gown hung from the lintel between the living room and the hallway. The last time I wore a poufy gown, I was the flower girl at Uncle José's wedding. In old pictures of me, I resembled an aqua cupcake. Abuela had made the miniature gown, and the first time I tried it on I struggled to get it over my head. It was a noisy dress and the tulle was itchy. A plastic crown of daisies sat askew on the top of my head. My frill-topped white socks drooped over my black patent-leather Mary Janes. I rustled loudly as I strewed rose petals down the aisle just ahead of the bride. Behind me, in the dusk of a Brooklyn wedding hall, the seventeen-year-old bride, sparkling in jewels and teardrops, floated to her groom.

At José's reception, Dad swooped me up to dance. My body went stiff and my legs hung straight down. He smelled strongly of something like disinfectant as he swayed and dipped with me off the beat of trumpeted Cuban music. Twenty-five years later, he was too stiff with Parkinson's to shuffle through a father-daughter dance at my wedding. I regret that we didn't at least try.

With cufflinks in one hand for his tuxedo shirt, Dad walked by my hanging gown every few minutes to finger the silk as if he could hardly believe that my nuptials were real. But I knew by the way he hovered that he also expected my mother to explode, as she always did when she was not the center of attention.

"Who knows if he'll show up," my mother said of Ken.

Later that afternoon a dozen roses of mazal for me arrived with a note that said, "I can't wait to marry you. I love you. Ken."

My hair was done, my veil pinned into place. I gave my mother one of my roses. "Be careful, there are always thorns," she said.

As we waited for our cue to walk down the aisle, my father stared straight ahead, gazing at yet another horizon. The huppah at the end of our walk seemed far away, as if I were viewing it from the wrong end of a telescope. The merry widow corset beneath my gown was too tight. My mouth was dry. I wanted to flee. I wanted to stay. I wanted to lean on my father, but he barely lifted his feet; his left arm trembled.

I gripped him tightly. Ken, our families, our guests were waiting.

"Is there anything you want to say to me before we take this walk?" I asked.

"You don't have to do this," my father said.

A few years earlier, on a yellowed index card my father must have palmed for his own wedding, I had found the transliteration of the words Jewish grooms have said to their brides for centuries. They were the same words Ken said to me under the huppah:

Judy Bolton and Ken Fasman at their October 19, 1991, wedding in Hartford, Connecticut.

"*Harei at mekudeshet li betaba' at zo k'dat Moshe v' Yisrael.*" With this ring you are consecrated to me according to the laws of Moses and Israel.

With that, Ken broke a glass to remind us of the tragedy of the ancient temple's destruction in the midst of our joy, and to symbolize the fragility of life. For me, the shattering of the glass has always been a reminder of how family secrets can devastate many lives; but at my wedding I allowed that moment to usher in a happily-ever-after emotion. I had a partner who deeply loved me, and who supported my curiosity as something important that gave way to worthwhile ventures. He was a partner who appreciated my need to excavate what brought my parents together and what kept them *pegado con chicle*, stuck together by chewing gum, despite the odds.

CHAPTER 15

The Ford Taurus

My father drove only American cars, keeping them longer than many marriages last. His final one was a gray Ford Taurus with a deep-red cloth interior. I had driven that car a few days before a police officer cited him for drifting between lanes and later revoked his license. I knew this was coming when I pulled the shiny, wine-colored shoulder harness across my chest and gagged on the stench. Something was very wrong. My father had been drooling, a common symptom of Parkinson's, onto the belt for months—and there it was, laid out before me, the unthinkable reality of losing him.

My father's driving made up so much of who he was. For years, he drove a shiny gold Duster for the State of Connecticut—the state seal emblazoned on the driver's side. Miles of road vanished beneath the wheels of his state car. He was the only driver in the household for years. He alone determined how and where we were going. He'd been the one to teach me to drive, but our time together in the car was often awkward. The car was my father's mobile confessional, in which he was the rambling confessor, and I, albeit self-consciously, took in everything he said.

The twenty-minute drive to my weekly violin lessons was his time to complain bitterly about my mother's family. "It stinks in there," he said of Aunt Reina's house. "They never open a goddamned window. They need fresh air," he yelled, his arm stretching out the window to pound the roof with his fist. According to him, fresh air was vital to a strong, functioning immune system and a healthy appetite. The winter air was particularly salutary.

I didn't dare remind him that, no matter the season, my aunt and abuela were deathly afraid of *microbios*—germs that they said made one terribly ill, germs that slipped in through window screens and air conditioners. Anyway, I liked the doughy, greasy smell of my aunt's house. If Aunt Reina opened a window, that odor of frying *buñuelos*—a Sephardic version of fritters—and the French fries that she emulated from McDonald's would sadly dissipate in the cold air.

"Greenhorns," my father further declared. I pictured rhinoceroses grazing in the fields of Saint Joseph College, their shiny horns a glinty green shade. I imagined that what rhinos and my relatives had in common was their thick-tongued existence in a foreign place.

"English!" my father screamed at his Cuban in-laws when they nervously whispered in Spanish. "Open the windows!"

When my father began to teach me to drive, his confessional monologues turned dejected. At a red light, I picked at the stuffing coming out of the Malibu's bench. Softly, sadly, he said, "I can't leave until you kids are grown and gone." By then he was tired of battling my mother and scolding her family, the family that insisted on deep frying food and speaking Spanish and keeping the windows shut against the vigorous, healthy cold air.

This was the moment in which my father's outrage plummeted toward defeat. "I'm so lonesome. I have no one else to talk to but you," he told me from the passenger seat, an admission that embarrassed me. At least I was close to getting my license and would no longer have to share those squirmy, cringe-worthy car rides. I was two months away from the precious solitude of driving alone at the speed I wanted to travel. I could soon make rolling stops without being accountable to my father, who could act like the most demanding traffic cop in the world. Two months from switching the radio from swirling string orchestras that played slow covers of everything from the Beatles to lively, fizzy Top 40. Two months from using the turn signals without having to add my father's archaic hand signals.

Soon after I got my license, Dad exhibited a creeping lassitude, the first of several signs of his Parkinson's. He was suddenly unable to drive long distances. His still-undiagnosed disease was becoming more noticeable as he walked with a distinct shuffle and his age-spotted hands trembled more and more. As a traveling auditor for the state of Connecticut, he requested assignments closer to home. "I'm afraid of changing lanes," he confided. "I don't know what's happening to me."

A series of ministrokes landed my father in the hospital a couple of years after I was married. His left arm shook uncontrollably. When he could catapult himself up from the wheelchair, he walked listing to the left.

By that time, I was newly pregnant. I sat up late with him in his hospital room, making note of the strong beat of his heart on the monitor. I wandered the halls to find someone to replace the empty IV bag, and came across a resident asleep at the nurses' station, a medical book version of *Parkinson's Disease for Dummies* lying face down across his belly.

A few months later, Dad was in the midst of several months of rehab at the Hebrew Home. I was huffing and puffing my way up and down the corridor as I pushed his wheelchair. "Hurry," he said. "The ship is boarding." He was sure that the supply ship on which he had served—on which he still thought he served—had docked in the Hebrew Home's parking lot. I almost believed him.

This was when he finally noticed I was pregnant. "My God, who did this to you?" he cried in astonishment. "You have to marry the fella right away!"

"I married him three years ago, Dad."

As I wheeled my father along the corridors, I tried to interest him in some of the Hebrew Home's events. Would he like to go to a sing-along? Would he care to discuss current events with one of the volunteers? He wanted none of that, mostly because his voice had become tentative and hoarse.

"How about if I read to you from *The Yale Football Story*," I said. It was my turn to read my old bedtime story back to him.

"It's a good one," he agreed.

My father had dipped into that book to tell me stories about characters like Albie Booth, Yale's 1931 football captain—Albie, the small but
fabled tailback nicknamed Little Boy Blue. At five foot six and 144 pounds,
the same as my father's height and weight in college, Albie Booth wasn't
the fastest player, but he was agile. My father so wanted to be Albie Booth.
He said Albie could change direction on the field without anyone notic-
ing until it was too late. My father was ten years old at the 1929 game
when Albie returned a punt and went on to score two touchdowns for
Yale. "I'll never forget it," Dad said each time he read the description of
the Yale-Army game to me.

His hand shook on my belly. The baby responded to his precarious
touch and kicked hard. She took my breath away. Every time she moved
the motion reminded me of a ship bobbing in a bottle, a replica of my
father's ship in the Pacific Ocean, the ship my father imagined had docked
just outside the doors of the Hebrew Home.

His hand still on my belly, he asked if I was carrying "a little boy blue."

"Or it could be a girl," I answered him. "We'll know in a couple of
months."

By the following fall, my father was a grandfather, for the first time, to my
baby daughter, although he was unable to hold little Anna without assis-
tance. He was leaving me, bit by bit, and I still didn't know this man. He
was home from rehab the following fall, and to spark any kind of conversation or revelation, I decided to listen to a Yale football game with him
through a wall of AM static on WELI, on the plastic Sylvania radio, its red
tuner yellowed with age. As I set things up on the porch, the anxiety and
the familiar sentimentality of trying to recreate my father's days of listening to the Yale games on the porch overcame me. I remembered how his
college buddies and Jack Laflin, the lone Princetonian, used to come over
to listen to the game. The Sylvania often had to stay in the hallway to
catch errant radio signals, similar to what I did for my Cuban relatives to
listen to Fidel. My father pumped up the volume so that Jack, and Kevin
Donovan, my father's college roommate, could hear the play-by-play. My

father poured Schaefer Beer in glasses he had chilled that morning. I knew his beer preferences and his love of Yale football well. I held in my heart the confessions he told me in the car. I would excavate his deeper secrets much later.

"I miss the Bowl," he said now, propped in a wicker chair on the porch. He refused to go to the Yale Bowl in a wheelchair.

I tucked in the corners of the red plaid blanket my mother had thrown over him. He fingered the fringes as if it were a tallit. "Scottish," he said of the blanket. My father liked to identify ethnicities. He was genuinely curious about where people came from and liked to guess at the origins of their names, an odd preoccupation for a man who all his life had tried to pass as pure American, free of any attachments to an old world. If Grandpa was modern, my father was post-modern.

As we listened to the game, Dad drifted. I tried to jar his memory, reminding him of "29–29," the score of the classic Yale-Harvard game. "You were there." Dad winced as if I had pricked him with a pin. He was dressed in sweats. White athletic socks stretched around his swollen ankles, and threadbare slippers dangled from his feet. His legs jackhammered beneath the Scottish blanket.

"Tell me the year," I continued to test him. I was determined that my father, the master of Yale trivia, would never forget the factoids that gave his life color and meaning.

"Nineteen-sixty-eight, the Harvard Coliseum," he rasped. "Lost the lead. Harvard scored sixteen points in forty-two seconds to tie it up."

"Harvard Beats Yale 29–29," blared the headlines. Harvard's comeback devastated my father all over again.

All of this happened the same year Bobby Kennedy and Martin Luther King Jr. were assassinated. There was deep unrest at the 1968 Democratic Convention in Chicago. People rioted in the streets of major cities. My father's resolute focus on Yale football was both a willful disregard of what was happening around him and a clue to his conservative politics, although I never officially knew the party he favored. He was a firm believer in the secret ballot. "You won't even tell me if you voted for Roosevelt?" I teased him. He was so tightlipped about so many of the subjects surrounding his life. My questions to him were always met with silence and a half smile.

As Dad's faculties diminished over the years, I frequently read Albie's story to him. It served as an improvised Kaddish for his New Haven boyhood, for the times with his father at the Yale Bowl. For as long as he could, with each mention of Albie's name, he'd lift up both arms and declare in a raw voice, "Touchdown!"

"Touchdown," he croaked when I held up the book so he could admire the big *Y* emblazoned on Albie's chest.

"Touchdown," he whispered every time he held his granddaughter, with my help.

"Touchdown," he said rallying, on the verge of saying more. But there was no more. There were only memories, forever tamped down in his soul and brain. Everything seemed gone. And yet, I kept looking for my father for many years; perhaps it was simply to tell him: I love you.

CHAPTER 16

The Wall

The Western Wall in Jerusalem is a place thick with desires and needs. The late Israeli poet Yehuda Amichai rhapsodized in "Jerusalem Ecology": "The air above Jerusalem is filled with prayers and dreams / Like the air above cities with heavy industry. / Hard to breathe."[4]

The Friday night before Passover, I was in Jerusalem to visit my best friend and for the first time to say the Kaddish for my father at the Wall. Prayer was indeed the "heavy industry" happening there—so heavy that I labored to breathe in the air as if I were asthmatic again. I longed for my father's old vaporizer to release me. I longed for his palpable presence amid the prayers colliding above me—prayers of the desperate, the pious, the righteous, the anxious. I choked on my own petitions for health, for luck, for prosperity.

Now 2007, it had been five years since I said a daily Kaddish for my father. I went to the Wall to pray and to say the Kaddish, which was by now a muscle memory. Dad was alternately near or gone. In recent months, he had disappeared from me. I was beginning to forget the sound of his voice, his lingering presence in my life. So on that night at the Wall I prayed to bring him closer.

---

4   Yehuda Amichai, *Yehuda Amichai: A Life of Poetry 1948–1994*, trans. Benjamin and Barbara Harshav, New York: HarperCollins, 1994.

I brought along the prayer book my father had received for his bar mitzvah. The book had an inscription to Dad dated 1932. The title page indicated that its publication had been in "Eretz Israel (Palestine)." Dad came across his prayer book almost half a century later, when he helped Grandpa move out of Stimson Road.

On the other side of the partition I espied black-hatted men—the kind of Jews my father considered throwbacks to a more decrepit world—as they moved their lips and swayed in prayer. Aside from the ultra-Orthodox backdrop, I sensed that my father would have been happy to know his boyhood prayer book had touched the same Wall that Moshe Dayan and his soldiers liberated from Jordanian occupation in the Six-Day War.

I had only recently reclaimed Dad's prayer book. Three years after he found the book in Grandpa's attic, I asked him if I could give it to Michael for his medical school graduation. I had already given Michael a stethoscope for Valentine's Day that year and we had taken turns listening to each other's heartbeat.

"He's practically family," I protested when my father was reluctant.

"I don't trust that fella," said Dad.

He was right. I gave Michael the prayer book and he vanished from my life with it soon after his graduation.

During many milestones in which I celebrated life and commemorated death, I ached for that missing prayer book. I wanted to read blessings from it at Anna's baby naming, and at my son Adam's circumcision. I wanted to read from it the first time I said the Kaddish at Dad's burial. When Anna and Adam received their own prayer books in elaborate ceremonies at their Jewish day school, it hurt to think that I had lost my father's book forever. As Anna's bat mitzvah loomed, I needed that prayer book to stand in for him, so I did what my doppelganger—Judy Bolton, Girl Detective—would have done: I tracked down Michael.

The Internet had become a crucial tool for sleuthing. It didn't take long to find him in suburban New York, and I had a good excuse for contacting him after twenty years: His father had recently died and my mother had seen the obituary in the local Hartford paper. I wrote Michael a condolence note in which I asked after the prayer book.

I wasn't sure whether he would write back, but he did. He said that for two decades he had carried the book from state to state, house to house. He said he always knew it belonged to me.

Returning a lost object, says the Talmud, is like restoring the soul of the person who lost it. Michael returned the book when we met over lunch in Boston. "I never should have kept it this long," he said. "It even made it through my divorce."

Holding it now in my hands in the Old City, a trip my father had dreamed of making, I wondered what the book meant to him. He couldn't read a single Hebrew word in it, but at Stimson Road he remembered holding it at his bar mitzvah with his parents standing on either side of him. There was no other book in the world for me to pray from on that Jerusalem Shabbat.

I noticed that on this trip to Israel, half a decade after my intensive year of mourning, some of the reading fluency I had acquired at the daily minyan had slipped away. Hebrew has at times been a touchstone for me. It is a language of energetic, sometimes chaotic, supplication. Yet there were times I pictured its heavy letters piling up in a graveyard and forming a language that only called up the dead. It was the language I associated with my early teen years at the Hebrew Academy. Over time, the letters became monochromatic to me—letters written in thick black ink, looking like abandoned buildings. Here at the Wall, I struggled once again to read through my father's prayer book.

I thought of the "paper tombstones" of writer Terry Tempest Williams. Her mother had bequeathed her six blank journals with not a shadow of a word on the pages. Yet, for Williams, and ultimately for her readers, they were anything but tabulae rasae, blank slates. In addition to paper tombstones, she imagined them as white flags of surrender, a white tablecloth not yet set, a scrim, a stage, an unwritten review. I envisioned them as blank invitations to create stories, to reunite with family again, and Williams must have felt the same way when she wrote that those blank pages contained words that were "wafting above the page." I imagined the words of the prayer book I held rising and then curling like my father's pipe smoke. I filled in the blank pages of his metaphorical journal by trying to piece his story together through my daily recitation of the Kaddish five years earlier. As that year of mourning went on, there were more and more blank pages to fill.

At the Wall, my father's prayer book was frailer than I remembered, the binding nearly unraveled, the front cover literally hanging by a thread. I looked through the thin, yellowed pages, careful not to tear them. There were the familiar blocks and blocks of Hebrew text with no relief of an English translation in sight. Did the unending typography overwhelm my father as well? Memories of my entreaties to God over my lifetime bobbed to the surface on the fragments of those dense black letters. My calcified Hebrew—hard, small shapes that my brain recognized but my lips could not altogether pronounce—was like the stones left after visits to the graves of loved ones.

I've always had some sort of dyslexia when it came to reading Hebrew. I frequently stumbled over the hulking letters as I tried to connect the Morse Code-like vowels underneath them. In Israel I was even more confounded when I discovered that the native speakers did not use those vowels when reading. They absorbed the language in large gulps. Hebrew, I quickly discerned, was so vital, so real, so different from my old and starchy associations with it. During my extended time in Israel, I came to feel as if I were on the verge of understanding the language.

Israel was also God's backyard, where Hebrew had been transformed into a modern language. It morphed into the utilitarian usage of street signs and restaurant menus. In the street names alone, Zionist icons mingled with medieval Jewish philosophers and biblical archetypes: Jabotinsky Street. Rambam Street. Queen Esther Street. Emek Refaim, one of Jerusalem's main drags, had a street name that was referenced in the Book of Joshua and Second Samuel.

For my parents, Israel represented the figure of biblical David, as in David and Goliath, and they cheered the country on as a beloved underdog that could prevail in any fight. It was the country where we sent the small change we collected in blue and white Jewish National Fund boxes to plant trees in honor of our grandparents, a gesture that delighted Grandpa Bolton. It was a land as fabled to me as Castro's Cuba was when

I was a child. Israel was far away, unattainable. The only way to get there was on an airplane my mother refused to take. It was the land of her lost love, the doctor who left her. It was the land she fretfully said we would escape to if ever a Holocaust happened in America.

When there was news about Israel on the radio or television, my parents shushed us, and when I was six years old my father seemed palpably shaken during the 1967 Six-Day War. During one of the summer nights of fighting in far-off Israel, he sat at the edge of my bed. "We need Israel to win this war," he said, adding softly, "Pray." It was an unusual request for him to make.

The closest he came to doing anything religious was to drop my mother and me off at synagogue services. But on that warm June night, at his behest, we prayed for Israel and her brave soldiers. It was startling that my father suddenly leaned on God so explicitly for a good outcome; until then I hadn't observed him rely on God for anything.

In my child's mind his prayers worked—Israel won the war in just six days. Perhaps my father's way to use prayer sparingly was potent after all.

My mother, clearly distraught over Israel's predicament in the early days of the war, still said the nightly Sh'ma with me. But this time we prayed harder, we implored further, we affirmed the Lord is God and the Lord is one. My father's faith was encapsulated in the odd, homespun piece of theology he adopted that went like this: God made the world, but the Dutch made Holland. This time, in Jerusalem, that aphorism translated as: God gave us Israel, but the Jews won back Jerusalem.

Throughout my season of memorializing, Israel was soaked in memory and transformed into the exclusive land of Kaddish. It was a haunted place and, for me, the eeriness of that time started at the Passover holiday.

From ancient times, Passover was designated as one of the three Jewish harvest festivals—festivals that later in the rabbinic period ended with the Yizkor memorial service. I pictured my ancestors floating, taking in the prayers and the pleas of the living, during such a service. After all, hadn't Margaríta and Josh told me in our otherworldly sessions that Grandma Bolton's spirit was sitting next to me?

Shortly after the Passover holiday, Israelis go on to remember their dead and their wounded as they commemorate fallen soldiers and Holocaust victims the day before Israel's Independence Day. My father was part of the generation that lived through the 1947 United Nations Partition Plan that established the Jewish state. He cherished Israel and no doubt would have admired the young Israelis—both men and women—wearing the uniform of their country. My mother, on the other hand, would have tried to seek out Manuel among the throngs of people in Jerusalem's center.

Israel is also a country of paradox. On Emek Refaim, I loved to people-watch from one of its many cafés, always amazed that there I was, the first in my original nuclear family to see Israel. Yet in one of those coffee houses, a chatty place of cappuccinos and strong Turkish coffee, there was a plaque in the entryway memorializing a twenty-year-old woman and her father who died there after a suicide bomber struck in the late 1980s. It had been the day before her wedding. Nevertheless, Jerusalem has always felt to me like the safest place in the world.

Women, however, are perhaps the most noticeable example of Israeli contradictions. Some are officers in the army, while others in the Haredi or the ultra-Orthodox communities sit in the back of public buses by decree of ultra-Orthodox men. At funerals women from all parts of society are banned from saying the Kaddish publicly. I thought of my father's funeral, where I not only said the Kaddish for all of the world to hear, I physically shoveled dirt onto his coffin, my tears mixing with the earth. My father was mine to bury.

In Israel, God is great. God is a bully. Jews are victims. Jews are occupiers.

In Israel, I set one foot in the country's Jewish narrative, the other in the Palestinian narrative. My best friend Susan's daughter was soon coming up on her army service and had been assigned to a base where eighteen- and nineteen-year-old women were in charge of Israeli intelligence. She would be among the young women who monitored the security barrier and the surrounding area. When I asked her about it, she told me, "It's a job just for girls because we multitask better than the boys."

My father would have loved seeing these young women snacking on potato chips in army fatigues while focusing on their monitors, blinking about as often as a guard at Buckingham Palace. Their workroom had to be uncannily silent. If a girl spotted a suspicious character by the barrier, she communicated to the soldier on the ground to pick up that person for questioning. The decision as to who warranted a closer look was hers alone. She arbitrated life-and-death situations several times a day. She was the one who guided soldiers if they had to crawl through brush and barbed wire to capture a suspect. If the mission went badly, hers was the last voice a soldier heard coming through his earpiece.

I went back to the Wall on another Shabbat evening to say the Kaddish for my father again, but I had to admit I was at a stalemate in my praying. I looked for Dad in Israel's prayer-saturated skies, but instead I was the tourist making shiva calls in Jerusalem that Amichai portrayed in his poem "Tourists": "They come here to visit the mourners. / They sit in Yad Va-Shem, wear grave faces at the Wailing Wall / . . . / They take pictures with the important dead at Rachel's Tomb / And Herzl's Tomb and Ammunition Hill."[5]

The women on either side of me were so fervent in their swaying back and forth to God's word, so practiced in the choreography of prayer, bowing and plowing through it like actors running their lines. Collectively they evoked the rhythms of minyans I had attended at Kehillath Israel and the Great Synagogue in Rome. Buzzy affairs, where the prayer train took off regardless of who had made it on board.

These women jostled for limited spaces up front, where they held their prayer books with one hand and placed the other on the Wall. I could not match their intensity, and stayed back and watched. A woman I had seen begging for alms on nonholy days stood next to me muttering prayers. She tugged at my arm—"You too tefillah," she said in her fractured English. She was giving me permission to pray, bestowing me with

---

5   Amichai, *Life of Poetry*.

the gift of speaking to God. I opened my father's prayer book and began. When I was leaving, careful to walk backwards from the Wall as tradition dictated, she slipped a bracelet of red thread with a tinny charm against the evil eye in my palm. These were the tokens she gave out during the week to people who spared her a shekel or two. "*Bracha*," she said. A blessing. I took it as the traditional expression: "May my father's memory always be for a blessing."

The moment was touching, but in the end there had to be more to mourning my father than visiting sobering tourist sites and drawing out the ritual of Kaddish to comfort me. It grieved me that Dad would always be a prayer away from me. I had to do something more, something dramatic, to find out who he was, but I had no idea what that would be.

"You have to find someone who knew him when he was younger," my friend Susan advised me. "He's always been this much older, unknowable man to you. Get to know him as someone other than your father. Get to know him as a young man. As someone's friend."

She was right, of course. But it just wasn't possible. All of his old friends were dead by now. I thought of his happiest times, of the picture of him in Guatemala that I had discovered as a little girl. I thought of the summer when he disappeared, unreachable, while we were in Miami. And there was Ana, the teenager who showed up on our doorstep, unexplained yet undeniably beloved by him.

"Sweetie, there has to be someone who's still alive," Susan said. "There has to be someone who can tell you about your dad."

I thought long and hard about who that person might be.

Part III

CHAPTER 17

The Lacerated Wedding Gown

I scoured my childhood for relatives and friends. I went over my parents' raucous parties in memory. There was the professor with three names who wrote the treacly poetry, or Yolanda Ramirez, who hosted Hartford's only television Spanish-language program, *Que Hay De Nuevo?* There was Jack Laflin, the potboiler writer. And there was always a crew of various South Americans. But I knew who would have answers for me.

It was Felipe.

My father was a different man around Felipe. I remembered the Sunday afternoons in Westchester, where the two of them made back-slapping toasts to each other in the backyard and leaned in as they spoke intently—and privately—while the burgers they were supposed to be flipping charred on the grill.

I scoured the Internet just as I had done to find Michael when I wanted Dad's prayer book returned. I typed Felipe's name in a search engine and nothing came up. I tried different spellings. I had to find him. The more I thought about it, the more I was certain that Felipe was the one man who had known and kept my father's secrets. My father had been his guest in El Salvador and the two had traveled together in Guatemala, but for all I knew Felipe was dead by now, too.

There aren't too many people these days who are scrubbed clean from search engines. They have to almost literally not know anyone in the world—which was not true of the voluble Felipe, patriarch of a large family. Or they have to be recluses, who neither go out in the world nor establish profiles of any kind online, not even for shopping.

Or they don't want to be found.

I was beginning to wonder if Felipe had ever existed at all, whether those Sunday barbecues were a figment of my imagination, when he suddenly popped up on a reunion list of his class at the Virginia Military Institute—complete with an email address. I wrote to him and a day later his enthusiastic reply landed in my inbox:

"Miracles do happen! How did you find me?"

It had been over twenty years since I'd last seen my father's old friend. Now it was 2008. The elevator to his apartment was as slow as the decades. His housekeeper let me into the living room of a whitewashed utilitarian apartment, a pied-à-terre in midtown Manhattan much like the ones I imagined he also kept in Miami and Buenos Aires. The only color in the apartment was concentrated in a massive oil painting of Felipe and his second wife, Leticia—blonde and dressy in pearls and blue ruffles, a dame with the bona fide English title to back it up. Leticia had died of cancer five years earlier.

The man who greeted me was slightly stooped and definitely elderly, in gray sweat pants and thick-soled sneakers. I had never seen Felipe wear glasses. He had aged into an amiable patrician, his hair sparse and white.

He took a few halting steps toward me. "This," he said of his limp, "is courtesy of a plane crash in Puerto Rico ten years ago." As head of an engineering association, he had been on his way to consult for a new university near San Juan when the plane crashed. Two of the four passengers survived. Felipe was flown to Walter Reed Medical Center, where he was reassembled.

As I hugged him, memories of those summer barbecues in his backyard washed over me. He stood back to hold me by the shoulders.

"You look so much like Harold," he said.

I wanted to cry. There weren't many people left in the world who could note the resemblance—although my mother always noticed it, not always with affection. My baby pictures were indistinguishable from my father's. "One face," she would always say, an indictment born of jealousy, as if my genetics had somehow displaced her in the line of succession to his heart.

One face. Everyone's story begins long before birth and goes on long after death, like a dead star still emitting light for a thousand years. Everyone arrives in this world trailing centuries of ancestors and stories. My story took off when my father—though older by society's standards for first-time fatherhood—was, to me, unimaginably young, and I was still stardust somewhere.

Felipe and I warmly caught each other up on the last two decades of our lives. I told him that I had lived in New York City until I wed in 1991, and in Baltimore for the first five years of my marriage. After I'd had Anna, and before giving birth to Adam, Ken and I moved north to Boston. Since I'd last seen Felipe in the 1960s, there had also been a graduate degree and travel, much of it pilgrimages to Jerusalem.

"I love Israel," he said. "The government there gave me an award."

"Wow, what kind?"

"Something to do with the Six-Day War," he said vaguely.

Felipe and I settled into conversation easily. We had many shared memories.

"It broke my heart to see Harold so sick, so incoherent," he said of my father's last days. "My only hope is that he recognized me."

Felipe was happy to reminisce about the old days when we were regulars at his house in Westchester, when he and my father often huddled in a corner in rapt conversation. When it came to exactly what they were saying to each other, he was less forthcoming. What had they been discussing? What had they been through together?

Felipe steered me away from this line of inquiry. "Remember when you hid and your parents didn't notice that you weren't in the car for almost an hour?" he chuckled. "Remember the time my sons almost drowned you in the backyard pool?"

Felipe's family of six kids always seemed a happy, mischievous brood, a handsome lot that looked like they could be in cereal commercials on

Saturday morning television. Maria Elena had been sturdy and kind—
not like my mother, who was always on the verge of whiteout hysteria. "I
wanted to get away from my parents," I told him.

"Your mother was a handful. Harold confided in me a lot about her."

"What did he say?"

"Oh, the usual."

I continued prodding. "You were his best friend," I said. "It makes
sense that he would tell you all about his trials and tribulations."

"He worried a lot about you kids. I know he was happy when you got
married and had your own family."

"I'm glad he was able to hold his grandchildren before he died,
although I'm not sure he understood who they were."

"I'd wager that he knew exactly who was in his arms."

Felipe appeared to be so certain when it came to my knowing my
father, but I had grown even more confused about Dad after his death,
despite the pains I had taken to try to reconcile myself with him. I told
Felipe about mourning my father with routine and purpose, about reciting prayers in his memory each day for almost a year.

"You inherited your religiosity from your mother," he said. "But she
could overdo it."

"It's as much about faith as it is about strategy for me."

"How so?" Felipe seemed genuinely interested.

"I started up with my Judaism in earnest when I mourned my father
for eleven months. I said a prayer called the Mourner's Kaddish."

"I have an idea of what that is."

"I said it because I felt Dad died without my ever knowing him. I have
never understood my mother, and I never really knew my father. They
have both been giant, looming mysteries in my life."

Both of my parents were enigmas—studies in contradiction. My
mother, both crazy and supremely ambitious; my father, militaristically
patriotic, yet a lover of Spanish and Central America. All I had about my
father were ambiguous theories. Clues like the ones offered in the *Hartford Times* word puzzle that I did with Dad every Sunday night, where
there were plausible reasons for both the right and the wrong answer.

"This is an either/or situation," Dad would say as we tried to work out the answers.

"Even though I was dedicated to saying the prayer every day, I think I've come as far as I can in knowing him," I said. "Something is still missing. That's why I've come to you. You knew him so well. I was hoping to hear your stories about him, about what he was like as a young man."

Despite my father's frequent warnings about how curiosity killed the cat, about how snooping could easily take a wrong turn, I was proud of my inquisitive nature. It was a way to consolidate power. But no matter how much I learned from going through his dresser and his checkbook, no matter how hard I tried to pray my way into his soul, silence surrounded my father like a force field. Felipe was my last and best hope of piercing that silence. I'd always had the impression that he and my father were more than just friends—that they had an abiding partnership of some sort. Between them there must have been so many trastiendas throughout the years.

"You want to know more about your parents; it's understandable," said Felipe. "More than they were willing to tell you." He sat in thought for a moment. "Perhaps you don't know the story about the time your mother threatened to kill Harold with a knife?"

This, I was not expecting.

"She did what?" I had managed to piece together bits of my parents' troubled courtship, based on the evidence of their bitter fights and their random love letters I found scattered throughout the house, but this episode was new to me.

Felipe proved himself a careful, deliberate storyteller. His account was like a recap of an old movie—black and white and crackling:

On the afternoon of Christmas Eve, 1959, while the businesses along downtown Chapel Street were emptying out for the glittering holiday, an unexpected visitor showed up at the staid New Haven accounting firm of Rosen & Rosen. The receptionist was already gone for the holiday, so one of the partners, my father's cousin David Rosen, opened the door for a young woman who was clearly in a state of great agitation. The girl's aunt trailed nervously behind, fanning herself with a train schedule. The pair had traveled to Connecticut from Grand Central Station, and before that all the way from Cuba.

The older woman was there for Matilde. And Matilde was there for Harold Bolton who, ten days earlier, had called off their wedding in Havana.

"Where is he?" Matilde screamed in her thick Cuban accent. Her B. Altman shopping bag ripped as she extracted a crumpled white silk gown. She took something else from the bag, too, and it gleamed silver: a butcher's knife.

Hijo de mala madre. Son of a bitch. Matilde said it over and over until she was breathless.

Her aunt, La Tía Estér, supported her in Ladino: "*Dio de la Zeda-kades.*" God of righteousness.

Hearing the commotion, Harold emerged from his office. There he found Matilde smoothing the handmade wedding dress against her body, as if to show how it would have looked on her. It was just the kind of troubling, erratic behavior that had made him back out of the wedding at the last minute—that, and his parents' appalled reaction to him marrying a Cuban girl almost half his age. I imagine my mother's Latina passion was part of the allure for Harold—a sturdy, only son of Jewish immigrants, whose parents, born in Ukraine, had insistently cultivated an American identity. But that afternoon, in the offices of Rosen & Rosen, Harold had no doubt that Matilde was capable of cutting herself, or even stabbing him to death.

Matilde had reason to be furious. What Harold had done had been uncharacteristically cowardly, even if for the best. He had long ago given up on the idea of marriage and, at forty, felt too old to start a family. Four months previous, Matilde had swept into his life like high winds and changed his mind, but his parents had helped him see reason again.

Meanwhile, the pressure on Matilde—particularly from her father, Abrahan—to marry must have been suffocating. At twenty-four, she should have been long married to make room for her younger sister, Reina, who was already engaged. Matilde had finally found her groom and went to Cuba to prepare for the wedding—until a Western Union telegram from his parents, translated into Spanish, arrived at Numero 20 La Callé Mercéd, just over three weeks before the December 20, 1959, wedding date: *Nuestro hijo no puede casarse con su hija, Matilde. La boda esta cancelada.* The wedding was canceled.

Matilde's mother, Elisa, had been pinning her daughter's wedding gown when Matilde read the telegram aloud. "Ay Dios," Matilde keened. Elisa nearly swallowed the pins. This was the darkest of bad luck. This was a curse.

Now, in the reception area of Rosen & Rosen, Matilde wrenched free of Harold's grasp as she dropped the butcher's knife and her gown crumpled to the floor. She knelt and tore off the brooch that strategically had been placed on the gown's neckline to hide just enough cleavage to satisfy her old-world father.

"Look at this," she wailed at Harold as she caressed the brooch. "It sparkles like the stars—the stars that line up to cause my misfortune!"

Matilde laid out the gown on the floor like the chalk outline of a murder victim. Now that she had Harold's attention, she slowly, deliberately, raked the dress with her knife, as if cutting long, raw tourniquets.

"I'm calling the police," Harold announced. He started dialing a black rotary phone that sounded hoarse, like a smoker. "The police," he repeated, pointing to the receiver. "*Policia*," he repeated for La Tía Estér's benefit. He was pretending the way he later did when I was a recalcitrant child and he claimed to have my teacher on the line.

Matilde was unmoved, but her aunt understood there weren't many options for an unstable girl from an unstable country. La Tía Estér was suitably worried as she shoved the mutilated dress back into the torn shopping bag—a bag whose exuberantly scripted B. Altman logo echoed the bold strokes of Harold Bolton's distinctive signature. With Harold now pointing the receiver at the two women like an officer's pistol, David Rosen herded Matilde and La Tía into the hallway and backed them into the elevator. "God help both of you," he said as the elevator doors closed.

Felipe's story stunned me. It went beyond anything I'd gleaned from my parents' old love letters, stashed in candy and cigar boxes in the dining room credenza along with sheets of S&H Green Stamps, waiting for me to discover them when I was a teenager. They were among the greeting cards congratulating my parents on my birth, and old anniversary cards my father had sent to my mother, signed "your Papito," her nickname for him.

My father's letters took me out of the polyester bell-bottomed '70s and into the white-gloved, pocket-handkerchiefed '50s of my parents, a place where Harold's lust for Matilde peeked through as love, although he occasionally referenced her tantrums. The first time I delved into that treasure trove, most of it in Spanish, I cringed at how awash in purple they were. My father wrote that he loved my mother "*con todo mi cuerpo*"—with his whole body.

Multiple readings later, I was inured to Harold's corny romance and was able to read the letters over, combing through for hints of the breakup that I knew was coming. I was on alert for mentions of Matilde's bad table manners, in which she didn't know a salad fork from a dinner fork; such sins presumably were bad enough to disgust Grandma Bolton. I studied the letters for mention of my mother's heart still showing cracks after losing her first and fiercest love, Manuel.

In the first letter that Harold wrote to the Estimada Señorita Matilde, he worried whether she had understood his American-shellacked pronunciation of Spanish when he made a date with her the week before in their mutual friend Violeta's living room. *En mi mente hay un pensamiento que yo pudé haber dicho a los doce en lugar de dos.* Perhaps I mistakenly said I would meet you at noon next Sunday instead of two o'clock. In later letters, Harold declared to Matilde in his clunky, earnest Spanish, "*Te quiero tanto con mi sangre, mi corazon!*" I love you with all my blood, all my heart.

Harold's bloated love letters were always penned in turquoise ink. In them he praised Matilde's beauty, her singing voice, her skin. The letterhead, which read K. Harold Bolton, 35 Stimson Road, New Haven, 11 Conn. USA, was splayed in a lavish stamped script that was the antithesis of my father's steady, precise, grammar-school printing. The return address, stamped in the grainy purple color of a mimeograph, was all business, yet across the flap of the envelope was the acronym SCUB—*Sel-*

lado Con Un Beso, sealed with a kiss—always in red ink and my father's print.

I rummaged through his awkward declarations of love until I came upon my parents' original wedding invitation, the wedding that was to have taken place in Havana.

"Where did you find that?" my mother gasped when I showed it to her. She frequently accused me of snooping on what I considered crucial fact-finding missions. I showed her the stash of letters I had unearthed. "This is my business," she said, aggravated. "You have no right to know my private life." Yet, the way she said it, teary and trembling, I knew she wanted me to know that my father had once loved her.

We had sat across from each other at the dining room, my mother with a mountain of Spanish tests to correct and I with an old invitation to a wedding that never happened. "Please," said my mother, beginning to tune into her anger, "I don't want to remember what your father did to me." And with that she grabbed the invitation and stashed it in her attendance book.

"Even with all their difficulties, your father was always a noble man," Felipe said to me.

"But, a knife?" I said. "Do you think there was something wrong with my mother?"

"We all did," he said. "You probably know that your father's parents, your grandmother in particular, was dead set against the wedding."

"Then why did they marry?"

Felipe threw up his hands. "Why did I have six children? Lust," he said. "It's always about lust."

Like any child, I didn't like to think of my parents falling prey to lust.

"Were you invited to the Havana wedding?" I asked.

"Of course. But that was not to be. I did make it to the small New York wedding at the large synagogue on Central Park West. There couldn't have been more than ten people there."

We talked like this for hours as I slowly gathered the courage to ask the one burning question I had come to ask, one I hadn't fully realized was the most important of all until I was sitting on Felipe's sofa. It was a question I'd had even without knowing what it was when I was little, one that turned into a joke among my siblings and me as we got older, one that seemed less of a joke as time wore on and our collective hunch began to seem reasonable.

"Felipe, please tell me—was my father a spy?"

He looked away, as if trying to find another story about my parents to distract me, but I believed that Felipe was *un hombre sincero* who at last would tell me the truth, the sincere man of the song I most associated with my mother—the song she sang at potluck suppers, sweetly and sadly to the soft strumming of a guitar.

Like José Martí, my father and Felipe were great patriots. They loved America fiercely, no matter what that love cost other countries—those in Central America, for example.

"*Digame por favor.*" Tell me, please. "Were you and my father in the CIA together?"

It had crossed my mind many times over the years, and each time I pushed the thought away. But what else could they have been doing together so often in suspicious Latin American locales? Why had my father doggedly stumbled his way through learning a language that didn't sit well on his tongue? Why did he persist in marrying a Cuban national when it went against both his parents' and his own better judgment?

Felipe was reluctant to answer. He seemed surprised I would pose the question at all.

He sighed. "Yes," he finally said.

I had expected the answer, and yet it sent me reeling. He rushed to explain: "Your father and I knew we had to stop Communism from spreading."

In my haze of hearing the truth confirmed at last, I missed the beginning of Felipe's story. I was heady with my success, and felt dread at how I would have to reimagine my father's earlier life, and what that meant for my family, and who I was.

And I have to ask you this question: "Did my father have a daughter named Ana in Guatemala?"

Felipe brushed aside my question.

But then he told me how he and Dad were in Guatemala working on behalf of the CIA to overthrow the Jacobo Arbenz government that existed from 1952 to 1954. My father, the loyal foot soldier, even carried a gun—a "gentleman's revolver."

"Think about it," Felipe said. "It was no coincidence that your mother was from Cuba. Your father needed to place himself in Havana in the middle of Castro's coup, and to place himself there in the most natural way. Your mother was the perfect cover. Who would doubt your Latinophile father's story that he had fallen for a young Jewish Cubana?"

"He married her just for that?" I asked, aghast.

"Not just for that," he said. "I told you, lust. And he had enough misgivings to cancel the first wedding, the one in Havana."

I tried to move on to all the questions suddenly bursting forth. "Was he gathering intelligence about the Bay of Pigs?" I asked.

Felipe smiled but stopped short of laying out the whole truth. "Insert your father into history and you will have the whole story," he said enigmatically.

CHAPTER 18

Freedom of Information

Felipe had confirmed that my father was a CIA agent, but what he told me explained everything and nothing. In the weeks after I saw him, I filed a number of Freedom of Information Act (FOIA) requests, but in response to everything I asked for came the same answer: the CIA would "neither confirm nor deny." This nonanswer came in letter-size envelopes sealed with thick brown wrapping tape.

I applied to the State Department for Dad's passport records and heard nothing back. I thought again of my fatherless summer in Miami after Castro hijacked the television screen night after night with his military bearing and breathless speeches, and wondered anew where my father had been all those times I'd tried to call Connecticut.

The Department of State assigned Mr. Douglas Jones to my case. His call came through on my mobile phone on my son's eleventh birthday.

Mr. Jones told me that he could not grant my request for my father's passport records. Through the Freedom of Information Act, I had written a letter to the State Department requesting "information about countries to which [my father] traveled on his United States Passport during the years between 1945 and 1960. I believe that he made several trips to Latin America, which may have included Guatemala, El Salvador, and Honduras."

"We just don't keep those kinds of records," Douglas Jones said. "Do you know whether he traveled for pleasure or on government business?"

His voice was sonorous. I was certain that requests like mine cluttered his desk. I pictured him with an American flag pin on the lapel of his nondescript suit. Was he saluting the red flags that my request had unfurled for his agency?

"I believe it was mostly government business," I said. I also believed that Mr. Jones already knew the answers to these questions.

"Was he with an agency, your father?"

For a long beat I didn't know whether to answer him truthfully. I felt as if I were confessing a deep, unspeakable secret.

"I have good reason to believe," I said, "that he worked for the CIA."

"Did he tell you as much?"

"Not exactly, although others have filled in some of the gaps." I didn't want to tell him about Felipe.

"Did you file a FOIA with the CIA?"

"I did. I also sent a copy of his death certificate, as per the instructions."

The Department of State also had a copy of Dad's death certificate, from which Mr. Jones read. "Let's see, born January 19, 1919. Passed on September 4, 2002, God bless him. Anyway, you probably won't find out much from the CIA. They're pretty tight-lipped over there. Do you know if your father had an alias?"

That hadn't even occurred to me. "Of the two of us, Mr. Jones, I think you would be more likely to know."

I could hear him shuffling papers on his end of the telephone. "I can certainly request your father's passport records," he said. "Would that be of help to you, Mrs. Bolton-Fasman?"

"It would, Mr. Jones."

"Can I ask why you are requesting this information at this this point in time?"

"I want to know about my father's life—his complete life," I said. "Even if it is posthumously."

"I see. Well then, Godspeed to you and yours."

I never heard from Mr. Douglas Jones again. He did not return phone calls. He did not send my father's passport records.

In the basement of Yale's Sterling Memorial Library it is always dusk. From a distance of sixty years, I squinted at the microfiche machine to read about Dad's war as it was recorded in the *Yale Alumni Magazine*. The day my father graduated, German troops had just begun occupying Paris, and an armistice to divide France among Germany, Italy, and the French Vichy government was in the offing. The American ambassador to the Court of Saint James's addressed the Class of 1940 about Britain's brave stance against the Germans.

Harold Bolton on a naval supply ship in the South Pacific, circa 1941.

The United States presented my father with a naval commission and orders to report to Officer Candidate School at the Brooklyn Navy Yard for three months of training in their program to give elite college graduates ninety days to absorb what midshipmen in Annapolis had four years to learn, or what lifelong military men learned over decades. My father the Ninety-Day Wonder skipped ahead of the line and was fast-tracked to become an executive officer of a supply ship. He departed his parents' boxy gingerbread of a house in New Haven for the Brooklyn Navy Yard in the fall of 1940.

A picture of my father, published in the January 1942 class notes, surprised me. In it, he has a moustache—the only time I'd seen him with facial hair—and is in naval dress uniform. If he harbored any insecurity about his swift rise through the naval ranks, it didn't show, because the photo presented an officer who expected to win the war. I wondered if this was the photograph that would have accompanied his obituary had he died in action.

The class notes of that year reported the war exploits of other classmates, too. Like Dad, they sent in pictures of themselves in uniform from Europe and beyond, handsome young men who looked older—the way people did in long-ago pictures—than their twenty-some years. From half a world away, the class notes indicated, Dad was en route to Australia, and still kept track of his beloved Elis on the gridiron. The scores came in for him over the teletype, and he rejoiced when Yale beat Princeton and Dartmouth. His enthusiasm for all things Yale must have irked the sailors; when someone doctored the Yale-Harvard score so that it looked as if Yale had lost, my father bothered to report to the magazine that he didn't fall for the prank, although his rah-rah Ivy League attitude inspired some of the sailors to call him Boola Boola Bolton.

In the class notes of March 1943, Dad noted that he had not seen American soil for almost three years. That casual mention implied that he was aiding the British in Greenland between 1940 and 1941, before the United States was formally in the war. He once told me how ironic it was that Greenland was full of ice, while Iceland was green and beautiful; it was his only allusion to that mission.

The notes go silent on Dad's life in the 1950s. There was nothing from him save the occasional report from a Yale football game, and then his wedding announcement in 1960. Now that I knew he had been in the CIA, I was looking for published confirmation of what he told me about "vacationing" in Guatemala or his accountant stint for the United Fruit Company, that notorious CIA front.

As a child, I thought it made perfect sense that my father had gone to his favorite vacation spot, a country where they spoke Spanish, and while there did some accounting work for the nice American company that imported tons and tons of his favorite fruit—bananas—to our shores.

A big company like that needed accountants, didn't they?

But the more I read about the history of Guatemala, the more I began to doubt my father's version of things. If he was involved in destabilizing the country, it might well have been through his connection to the United Fruit Company. Gabriel Garcia Marquez captured the brutality that the United Fruit Company foisted on their workers. In his novel *One Hundred Years of Solitude*, Garcia Marquez writes about the 30,000 banana workers who went on strike in Colombia to demand better working conditions. The Colombian military then went in and killed a thousand unarmed strikers and their families in the town square of Ciénaga after Sunday church services. In perfect pitch, A character in Garcia Marquez's novel blasts what went wrong in Latin America: "Look at the mess we've got ourselves into just because we invited a gringo to eat some bananas." My father was one of those banana-eating gringos.

When Jacobo Arbenz was democratically elected as Guatemala's president in 1951, one of his main goals was to redistribute the country's massive amounts of fallow land among its peasants. The United Fruit Company was having none of it. Arbenz was determined to establish his political independence. Large estates and private farms were in the hands of a few, and Arbenz meant to transform Guatemala into an economically independent country. From there it was not a big leap to buy into a creaky notion that Arbenz was a Communist. A public relations campaign painted Arbenz, who was an idealist and admirer of Franklin Delano Roosevelt, as a screaming red Communist. The accusation sailed through Congress, and perhaps most notably it was the accusation that placed the CIA on the ground in Guatemala.

My father made his way into the middle of this turbulence, convinced that his presence was wholly needed, wholly patriotic. He and his pal Felipe apparently participated in a US-backed coup called "Operation Success." Given what I learned about Guatemala's troubled history, it was the first time that I questioned my father's commitment to a pure notion of democracy. My father was not a man who dealt with abstractions. He heard what he heard, and he saw what he saw, and that was his truth. But his naïvete, and his unquestioning belief that there was a Communist beachhead in Guatemala, were striking to me. The question was not so much what my father had done in Guatemala, but whether he had had a direct hand in creating the power vacuum that right-wing death squads were only too happy to fill.

Operation Success was put into motion to replace the government, and in 1954 the CIA eventually sent a confused, broken Arbenz into a diaspora where no one wanted him. He wandered the globe looking for a place to settle down. Places like Cuba, Uruguay, and Russia offered him no solace. Addicted to pills and alcohol, he died in Mexico City in 1971 at the age of fifty-eight, inebriated when he drowned in the bathtub of his hotel room.

I wonder if my dad kept track of Arbenz's sad, jumbled exile. Did he read about Arbenz at the same time he read the Sunday comics in our den? Did he keep the news he had gleaned of Arbenz to himself or did he make a whispered telephone call to Felipe? At that point, what happened in Guatemala would have been so long ago. My father was no longer an active agent. And yet I am sure these experiences of their young warrior days stayed with them. The silence that followed what happened in Guatemala shaped my father's time. Talking was not an option when he was young. Talking was painful when he was an old man. Felipe's description of my father as a "noble man" rang in my ears like the twang of a guitar string. And, given what I was learning about the CIA and Guatemala, Felipe's description confused me.

I grew restless and agitated while hunting for my elusive father among the black-and-white reels of microfiche. He was turning out to be a Zelig-like figure in modern Latin American history and beyond. I switched tactics and decided to search for Jimmy Rosen in the Yale alumni notes for the Class of 1921.

Jimmy Rosen was the cousin with whom I shared two initials—he was James Frederic to my Judith Frances. He had, according to Harold Bolton, a crackerjack mind and idiosyncratic humor, and stayed continually alive in my father's imagination, eventually taking up permanent residence in Harold's Parkinson's-addled brain. I thought that perhaps Cousin Jimmy might have something to convey to me posthumously about Dad. I was convinced there was more to Jimmy's story than anything I could deduce from my impressions of his old photograph.

I was sure Yale's Sterling Library contained his story—facts discovered in staid libraries of wood and paper, with fluorescent lighted basements and backlit screens of microfiche machines. I tried not to assign too much superstitious significance to the coincidence that Jimmy and I shared the same birthday. I pored over the notes to reconcile Jimmy the prankster with the childless labor attorney he became, looking for hints of a story that my father once told about Jimmy's temporary disbarment for placing his enemies on Communist-party mailing lists, going far beyond "prankster."

According to the yearbook, James Frederic Rosen was born in 1899, on the cusp of a new century, in Galveston, Texas. His parents, Morris and Dora, were part of the wave of Jewish immigrants from Russia who came to the United States through the bustling port of Galveston. Jimmy, the first-born son, was the progeny of an uncle who married his niece; Grandma Bolton used to say that those particular Rosens were not right in the head, that there was "too much of the same blood" among Jimmy and his siblings. His brother Julius was a piano prodigy who spent much of his adult life homeless, and his sister Evelyn turned out nervous like Grandma.

Morris and Dora opened a dry goods store in Galveston. A butcher by trade, Morris hung logs of salami and bologna in the window. The Rosens eventually moved to Fall River, Massachusetts, where Morris was once again a butcher. With Jimmy's admission to Yale, the family finally settled in New Haven.

I stared long and hard at Jimmy's yearbook picture. I noticed the left eye, the glass eye. The story came back to me about Jimmy poking his eye out on a tree branch when he was nine years old. When I was the same age, Jimmy's story was a cautionary tale for my wild behavior. "You could lose your eye just like Cousin Jimmy and we'd have to put a glass marble in the empty socket," Dad would say. I imagined a glass eye as blue and patterned as the pictures of Earth I'd seen beamed to my television screen from the Apollo spaceflights.

Decades of the *Yale Alumni Magazine* went by in a blur. There was something so satisfying about the scratchy whirr of the microfiche as I occasionally stopped the machine to land on advertisements from the '30s and '40s for the clothier J. Press. There were laundries that pressed shirts for the young gentlemen of Yale University who always went to class in tie and jacket, and I thought of a memoir I had read about a relatively recent Yale graduate who ironed his classmates' clothes for pay. Everything and nothing had changed.

I threaded and rethreaded the microfiche for hours to read the Class of 1921 and the Class of 1940 notes up through my father's death in 2002. Both Dad and Jimmy had been avid contributors. As I read, it occurred to me that they wrote so frequently as a way to fit in with their true-blue Yale brethren; Jimmy, in particular, was a Jew who didn't have the same pedigree as his classmates, while Dad was a legacy admission at Yale with a surname that didn't sound Jewish.

In 1942, K. Harold Bolton was a young naval officer in the middle of a world war, struggling to stay in charge as the executive officer of a supply ship somewhere in the Pacific Ocean; yet he paused to reflect on his mortality by writing for the class notes, "I will be a Yale man until the day I die."

Dad once told me that Jimmy Rosen frequently dropped him a line during the war. I asked my father what happened to those letters, but he said they vanished, as if they had become a different form of matter. In the letters that Dad sent back home to his father, he mostly talked about Yale football; he knew the statistics, the players, the logistics for every game Yale ever played. But his back and forth with Jimmy must have been different in content and tone. The nineteen-year age difference between the cousins made Jimmy not quite young enough to be like an older brother and not old enough to be a father figure. Nevertheless, the cousins were extremely fond of each other. Jimmy admired Dad's prodigious memory and might even have encouraged his young cousin to barge into his sister's sweet sixteen party and recite the capitals of all forty-eight states. Or maybe Jimmy loved music as much as Dad and was proud of his young cousin's encyclopedic knowledge of Viennese waltzes, light opera, and patriotic music. Dad told me he admired Jimmy's offbeat sense of humor—like when Jimmy popped his glass eye out in front of Grandma, nearly causing her to faint. He scared my cousin Betsy when she was a teenager home alone by phoning her to say he was a dead relative coming to get her.

"That's the Rosen sense of humor," Dad said, although I didn't understand what he found so appealing about it. My father was probably disappointed that I turned out to be a dour little girl who couldn't deliver the punch line of a joke. I sat stony-faced before *Laurel and Hardy* and the *Three Stooges* as my father roared with delight.

In his class notes during the '40s and '50s, Jimmy wrote that he frequently left his wife, Lillian, at home during business trips. For example, in 1952 he went without her on an all-expenses-paid junket to Mexico and Central America. In an otherwise dull afternoon, this piece of news blared at me from the microfiche. According to Felipe, he and my father were already in Guatemala at that time on behalf of the CIA: "Guatemala 1952," said the scallop-edged photo of my dad, the bumbling gringo tourist in the pith helmet. Jimmy was too old to serve during the Second World War, and his glass eye surely would have disqualified him, but it wouldn't have counted against him for intelligence work, and he was just as patriotic as my dad. It seemed more than coincidental that my father and his all-time favorite cousin both happened to be in Central America on "business" at the same moment. Had Jimmy joined Dad and Felipe at the United Fruit Company, perhaps on retainer as a lawyer who could help their public relations effort to consolidate public opinion in their favor against the Communist threat? Through the class notes, was he trying to telegraph his importance to national security? It wasn't as if he were casually reporting on a glamorous family vacation the way his classmates did.

A thought occurred to me.

Perhaps it was the other way around. Perhaps Jimmy Rosen was the one to recruit his smart-as-a-whip cousin, the kid with uncanny recall, for the Office of Strategic Services.

I imagined Felipe, Jimmy, and my father in Guatemala—the two younger men working in the trenches gathering information, mingling with the locals as they fantasized about living a spy life that clumsily imitated a James Bond novel or one of Jack Laflin's formulaic spy stories. Those dime store paperbacks were Jack's bequest. He had no heirs, but there was a rumor that he had a son in Hawaii serving a long jail sentence. Both he and his wife struggled with alcoholism, although he was more functional than she was.

What was with these men and their secret lives? While my mother's great wish had been to be the proud owner of a built-in vacuum cleaner, my father and his closest buddies were flirting with spy-dom.

To get a better picture of what the spy life might have been like, I had recently picked up one of Jack's pulpy novels. I had only ever known him as my father's friend, which is to say I didn't know him very well, but his voluble presence at my parents' parties had made him hard to ignore. As I got older, I noticed he flirted with my straightlaced mother, who was both flattered and scared by the attention. My father had adored him— even though Jack was as crazy for his alma mater, Princeton, as Dad was for Yale, bragging he owned a toilet seat with a Princeton seal on it. He had majored in Spanish after flunking economics.

Of Jack's handful of published books, I read *The Spy in White Gloves*, part of a trilogy about the Latin American adventures of tough-guy spy Gregory Hiller, who, it became clear, was the desperately wished for alter-ego of Harold and Jack—and maybe Jimmy, too.

The character of Gregory Hiller is a rake, a seducer of buxom women, and also handy with manly-sounding firearms. This Latin-savvy James Bond enjoys sexual escapades that defy probability: in one situation with a beautiful yet lost soul, they "experienced together the delights of the love act, reaching a shattering communal climax that left them gasping and drained." It reminded me of the time Jack once declared, oddly, in alcohol-soaked words at one of my parents' parties: "I want to come back in my next life as a high-priced call girl."

I had never known how Jack and my father found each other in Hartford, Connecticut. Harold didn't pick up new friends easily. In the only picture I have of the two of them together, Dad in a three-piece suit holds a can of Heineken, an uncharacteristically fancy beer for him, and Jack has a glass of liquid that is undoubtedly a strong gin and tonic. I had seen other pictures of my father raising a glass to the moment; I found one such photo in his highboy, taken in his college days, where he is toasting a young woman. I was on one of my reconnaissance missions, and I brought the picture to my mother, who immediately ripped it in half to erase the other woman's image.

Did my father look back on his spy days as if he'd been Gregory Hiller—a character Jack was desperate to portray as debonair, even heroic, in his hyped-up, nicotine-stained prose? A character who didn't hesitate to use a gun to bring about world peace, one continent at a time? "Your father carried a gentleman's revolver," Felipe had said.

In *The Spy in White Gloves*, Jack dispatches Hiller to go undercover in San Rosario, a fictitious South American backwater near Uruguay that made Sodom and Gomorrah look like Disneyland. "Could there have existed a place where human life was held in such total disregard as San Rosario?" Hiller muses to himself rhetorically. "Death was a frequent visitor to the jungle pesthole."

Fidel Castro's malevolent spirit hovers over the pages of the book. Felipe had said that he and my father knew they had to stop the spread of the Communism in Latin America; in the CIA's estimation, Castro was gaining a foothold in the region and had to be stopped. Gregory Hiller echoes that theory when he opines: "A Sovietized Cuba a mere ninety miles away from the United States soil was revolting enough; the concept of a Latin American continent under the hegemony of Moscow, even indirectly, was unthinkable." It was the same dictum that Felipe had professed, and it also called up his insinuation that Harold married his young Cuban bride as part of his patriotic job description.

I initially shrugged off Jack's version of the spying life in Latin America until I saw it for what it was: the swashbuckling fantasy he and my father must have thrived on. It was a life of coded knocks, dark sticky bars, theories spilled in hushed tones along with warm beer, hard drinking, white dinner jackets required at feasts, and even orgies. In Jack's made-up world, "a tremendous quantity of alcohol was being consumed in a wide selection of forms—champagne, scotch, gin, various wines. Servants constantly replenished the supply, circulating among the throng of guests with fully laden trays. The buffet: caviar, ham, turkey, pheasant, lobster, whole roast pigs, viands at whose identity Hiller could only guess—all were being consumed greedily, in fantastic quantities." Their version of owning a built-in vacuum, I supposed.

As for "the various acts of perversion, even the sophisticated Gregory Hiller was shocked." This was a far cry from the boozy yet relatively tame potluck dinners my parents threw in West Hartford. The sexiest thing that happened at these soirees was when someone strummed a guitar to accompany my mother as she sang soulfully in Spanish. Any thought of debauchery—if there was any—stayed tightly coiled and buried.

And yet, there were glimmers of my father's old life even in something as everyday as his increasingly shabby wardrobe. His J. Press shirts had fraying collars. His golf clothes were ghosts of themselves, his khakis washed many times over. The cleats on his golf shoes were worn down, and the brown and white shoes had been spruced up with sticks of white polish over the years. Did Dad fancy himself as a Gregory Hiller type? *Amor, salud, mujeres y tiempo para gosarlos.* Love, health, women and the time to enjoy them, like his old toast with Felipe.

Hiller readily admits that spying was ninety-nine percent waiting, one percent action. Did my father, Felipe, and Jack while away ninety-nine percent of their time in pursuit of that one percent adrenaline high? Is that what really drove them, beyond patriotic fervor? I tried to envision what such a high would look like. Would they garner information in a nefarious bar like the Golden Bird with its "babble of voices, clink of glasses, occasional snatch of drunkenly discordant song?" The bar in the novel sounded more like a clichéd movie set than a functioning waterhole where actual espionage took place. Did a democratic outcome for Latin America depend on a faithful go-between, like the happy native Luis de la Torre? In spite of myself, I got caught up in Jack's pulpy imagination. No matter that I knew the place was ridiculous—it still had an old-world glamor that my father must have known well at some point in his life. I imagined Jimmy Rosen in charge of the Guatemala operation, impatiently waiting in a hotel room in Guatemala City, his San Rosario.

Spending time in the minutiae of my father and Jimmy's class notes made me fidgety. I needed air. Outside, the February day was postsnowstorm gray with a creeping chill. I called Felipe for what I hoped would be a reality check of the story I had spun—a story that in its own way was as fantastic as fiction.

"I'm at Yale reading through class notes," I told him. My breath came out in plumes of vapor-like fog. I asked the question without any preamble. "Did you know my father's cousin Jimmy Rosen?"

"Never heard of him."

"Jimmy wrote that he was on a junket to Latin America in 1952. Was it Jimmy who recruited my father for the CIA?"

Felipe was initially curt, then annoyed. "I can't tell you any more than I already have," he said.

"Okay, but was he one of your contacts for the mission in Guatemala?"

At this point, I didn't think it was prudent to also ask him about Ana.

The other end of the phone went silent, although Felipe had not hung up. I felt like a psychology experiment in which Felipe would feed me bits of information and wait to see what full-blown theory I spun from them.

"You told me to put the pieces together," I said. "You told me what Dad did made sense in the light of history."

"It was a perfect set of circumstances," Felipe finally said. "A mainframe computer somewhere spit out your father's card. Go through his credentials and you'll come to understand. It makes much more sense than your cousin theory."

"But the cousin theory doesn't contradict what you said about Dad being the right man for the CIA."

Felipe's silence, followed by his creaky denial, made me all the more certain I was right—that Cousin Jimmy had been a spy, the one who had first indoctrinated and mentored my father.

It might have been a leap, but I felt it was a logical one, and I was heartened by how Felipe did not exactly deny it, even if he wouldn't corroborate it, either. Like the CIA's response to the Freedom of Information Act requests I had filed, he would neither confirm nor deny.

"I need to see you again," I said to Felipe. It had been several months since our watershed meeting.

"That might be difficult to arrange," he said. "I feel lousy. I have cancer"—he pronounced the word cancer with an emphasis on the second syllable, in Spanish. "It's in my blood."

I was shocked, and told him I was sorry. But I didn't let go. I had waited so long for this information, felt so close to getting it. Felipe was the key. I told him I had a right to know my father's story and that he had an obligation to tell me.

He hung up on me.

Back in the library, the microfiche was still on, cued to the same place where I'd left it. I cried the frustrated tears of a child as I unspooled the film.

CHAPTER 19

The Duchess

As soon as I introduced myself on the phone as Harold and Matilde Bolton's daughter, Violeta's recognition was palpable through the receiver.

"Your parents stayed married?" she asked in disbelief.

The last time I saw Violeta, she had had us all over to her house in Miami, where my newly reunited parents were already in an argument right there at her dinner table. Between servings of Violeta's spicy picadillo, my parents took up the fight they'd been itching to have in the car on the way over.

"We need to go home," my mother said, her hand squeezing my father's knee. She was tired of living in hotel rooms, even the nice one we had now that my father had returned from who knew where.

"I'm a step ahead of you," my father said. "I've booked our flights for the day after tomorrow."

My mother removed her hand from his knee. Her eyes turned to ice. "You know I don't fly."

"It's the twentieth century," he said. "Everyone flies."

"Mommy, I want to ride in an airplane!" said John. I, too, was excited at the idea of flying through clouds and looking down on a map-etched world.

"You know I don't fly," my mother repeated, her voice rising to a scream. "How could you betray me like this? You're trying to trick me, Harold Bolton, and it won't work. I will not set foot on an airplane. I will not allow these children to set foot on an airplane. *No tienes ni una gota de respeto*." You don't have a drop of respect for me.

To highlight my father's latest sin, my mother emphasized the word *gota*. It was one of her more descriptive words. Everything she fought for, everything she wanted took *gotas* of her blood, *gotas* of her sweat and tears.

Violeta's husband, Arthur, shepherded us kids into a bedroom. "They'll stop," he promised. "It's just a misunderstanding."

Through the crack in the door I saw that my parents had assumed their familiar still-life posture—my mother weeping with her hands over her face and my father standing over her, balanced precariously between rage and confusion.

My mother rode to the Colonial Inn in the back seat between my brother and me. I held her hand to keep her from jumping out, although she looked too exhausted to make her usual vehicular threat. Carol in the front seat held a gritty beach pail in her lap in case of carsickness.

My mother's scent was a mixture of Maybelline and desperation. It was the first time I understood that she could actually abandon me. Yet, with her head resting on my shoulder, I also understood how much she needed me.

My father was fifty and drained. It was a turning point. He could no longer keep my mother's demons at bay.

He had finally surrendered to her volatility. A week later, we were back on the Silver Meteor, this time heading north.

At Penn Station in New York we transferred to a Hartford-bound train. As much as I had missed Hartford, pulling into the city's Union Station did not feel like a homecoming. I felt landlocked as I became keenly aware that there was no longer an ocean to which I could walk. After my mother's initial fear of beach and sun, Miami had become a city of strolling and convenience for us. Everything we needed, everything we ate was a walk away at the Rexall and the Cuban diner. Lincoln Road was a colorful Spanish version of downtown.

Now Hartford was lonely after we had crammed ourselves into living rooms with Estersita and Victoria and the assortment of relatives that came with them, united in both our repulsion for and anticipation of

Fidel amid the television's electronic blizzard. Back in Connecticut, we spent Sunday afternoons in Grandma and Grandpa Bolton's pristine house, where the housekeeper waxed the furniture to a high sheen until I saw my reflection.

Mostly I spent stillborn afternoons in the backyard that Dad liked to brag was technically more than an acre. Within the yard's square boundaries was an acute absence of the Atlantic Ocean's limitlessness.

In my Connecticut backyard I paced the perimeter like a trapped animal. The canopy of the tall, sturdy maple trees was more suffocating than shady. Afraid that someone would kidnap her children, my mother sat on a beach chair in the backyard keeping vigil with a wet washcloth on her migraining head. Her overprotectiveness had been one of the chief things that distinguished us as the crazy *I Love Lucy* Latinos of West Hartford, but the summer we came home from Miami I was irreversibly Latina in language and preferences. Dreary Connecticut was quickly closing in on me. My world had changed—a world as erratic as the television signal that brought a speechifying Fidel Castro to the screeching group of Cubanos in Estersita and Pepé's living room. I had a deep tan. "You look like a *negra* from Havana," Abuelo said.

More than four decades later, I Googled my way to Violeta. It turned out that a few years after introducing my parents at her baby shower in Brooklyn, she and her husband, Arthur, had moved to North Miami Beach.

She was now eighty-one years old. She told me she had trouble recalling things, but the mention of my parents' names certainly jogged her memory. For Violeta, who introduced my parents, hearing their names again was like calling up well-known duos—from Bonnie and Clyde to Ginger and Fred. Despite my parents' difficulties, there was an inherent coupling, a natural history that their names evoked when mentioned.

I wanted to know if Violeta had her own version of my mother's near-homicide with the knife and the wedding dress—and, of course, whether she knew my father had been in the CIA. Anything she could tell me, I wanted to hear. But my questions were too complicated; her memory turned as murky as the basement of 1735 Asylum when it flooded after a storm. It became clear that it would be futile to ask her about my father's friendship with her brother Ramón. At the same time, I was afraid that if some of the secrets she swore not to tell lit up her hippocampus, being too direct with her might push her to hang up on me as Felipe had.

"It's a miracle they stayed married," she repeated. "Do you remember Arthur taking you into our bedroom when they were fighting at the table?"

I did, and thought about how different my own children's lives were—how hard I'd worked to spare them such trauma. They have never snapped awake in the middle of the night from hearing their parents yelling or crying. They have never known the bright red pulsating light of a police cruiser illuminating their nighttime bedroom.

I changed subjects, hoping the switch was not too abrupt or disorienting for Violeta. "Tell me, how did my father meet your brother Ramón?" I asked.

"Ah," she said. "Ramón had a store in New Haven." She could not remember the location or even what Ramón sold; she only knew that my father loved to practice Spanish and that he had a wide circle of Cuban friends in Connecticut. She remembered there was a Cuban Club in Bridgeport to which he belonged, "a social place. He met women there, too. Your father had a lot of Cuban girlfriends, but your mother was the youngest and prettiest."

I readied myself to tell Violeta that I was certain my father had been in the CIA, that he'd been a spy. She had known him in those days and might acknowledge the truth.

"Here's why I'm calling, Violeta," I began. "I recently found out that my father was in the CIA."

"What's that? The CIA?"

"The Central Intelligence Agency. I imagine that he also recruited other agents. It would have been useful if those agents were native Spanish speakers. Do you think he pulled Ramón into the CIA, too? Does that make sense? Can you remember anything about that?"

Violeta was quiet. I held back from filling up the dead air with more questions. I knew better than to quiz a person with a failing memory.

She remembered nothing about Ramón possibly being in the CIA. She mentioned the club again, "a social club."

"Tell me," she finally said, still stuck on one track. "How did your parents stay married for all those years?"

Come to think of it, how *did* they stay married?

Three months after the botched attempt at a formal wedding in Havana, my parents were improbably back together. My mother's version was that Harold telephoned her on Valentine's Day 1960 and asked her again to marry him. He told her he missed her and that he wanted to start a family with her. A month later, my mother marched down the aisle of the Spanish-Portuguese Synagogue, skirting the annulment my father initially wanted after their civil ceremony.

After all of my FOIA disappointments, I wanted any kind of documentation I could hold in my hands. It was the easiest thing in the world to write to the Bureau of Vital Statistics in New Haven to request my parents' marriage license. As I held the envelope they sent, I paused over the odd juxtaposition of those two words—*Vital* and *Statistics*. Coupled, those words described my quest for stories of my parents, a desire to know that there was an actual marriage recorded in black and white, not just stories of near-annulments and near-homicides. Later I would find out that my parents obtained a second marriage license in Brooklyn in early March 1960.

I read and reread the license, looking for signs of the wedding in Cuba whose cancelation came the following month. The flimsy piece of paper was part of the documentation to prove my parents had wed at all.

Throughout her life, my mother has had a complicated relationship with official documents. She was known as Miss Matilde Alboukrek when she signed the marriage certificate. It listed that she was born in 1935, which she claimed was a mistake. "My father didn't register my birth until I was twelve," she insisted. "I was born in 1936."

There was also her insistence that she was a direct descendant of the Duke of Albuquerque in Spain; she claimed that the name Alboukrek was a tweaked version of Albuquerque. I have no doubt that she offered her regal explanation to the clerk at the courthouse.

My four grandparents appeared on that marriage certificate, too, making it a historical document for me: Abrahan, Elisa, William, Anna. "Turn it and turn it again, for everything is in it," says the Mishna, a compilation of Judaism's oral law.

There must have also been a *ketubah,* or marriage contract. When I asked to see theirs before my own wedding, or to know who had witnessed the metaphorical agreement between them, neither of my parents remembered where it was. There was only the smudged, secular, black-and-white proof that once there had been love, which was then lost—hemorrhaging like blood after a miscarriage.

For all my contemplation of their wedding certificate, the gaps in their twisted marital history only widened, questions looming like a thundercloud. In my mind's eye I saw again the telegram my grandparents sent to my mother, which I found on a fact-finding raid in my parents' dining room credenza. *La boda esta cancelada*—the wedding is canceled. Then there was the story that Felipe told me about my mother shredding her gown with a butcher knife. As for the rest of my parents' story, I filled in the spaces with theories and suppositions. As Felipe suggested, there was lust. There was also my father's desperation to settle down and start a family, and my much younger mother was available and more than willing. There was the convoluted history of my parents' two out of three marriage ceremonies.

As I pieced together their story, it occurred to me that my father was like the protagonist of the Graham Greene novel *Our Man in Havana.* He was the New Haven, Connecticut, version, attempting to place himself in Havana, albeit in a roundabout way. Or maybe he was the original Gregory Hiller, packing heat in a jungle-hot hell on earth.

My father the groom signed his marriage license with that familiar flourish: K. Harold Bolton. The *K* anchored Dad's signature, followed by an illegible tail of script meant to be read as "Harold Bolton." *K* stood for Kenneth, the name that Dad never spelled out, never used. A spook of a name. People always simply called him Harold.

As our phone call went on, Violeta became more confused. "The week of your parents' honeymoon, your grandmother stayed with me and sewed bathrobe after bathrobe, all of them in pink," she said. But before I ended the call, I again addressed the question hanging between us.

"No, I don't know anything about the CIA," Violeta said. "I only know that your father loved the Cuban people."

That was the best Violeta's poor memory could offer. Perhaps it was enough.

CHAPTER 20

Seeking Ana

In my living room hangs a portrait of Tía Rashél, my abuela Elisa's older sister. Photographic in its intensity, emitting loneliness and longing, the lithograph captures a pocked and wrinkled woman, rivulets of sadness and trauma running across La Tía's smallpox scars. Her namesake, my cousin, is the gifted artist who captured La Tía Rashél in all her Sephardic gothic majesty. It is a portrait of angst and shattered love. Her face carries the story of her husband abandoning her when her dowry did not come through, even though she was already pregnant with their first and only child.

Tucked away in the attic is a framed portrait of my great-grandfather the rabbi, Abraham Rosen. It more than represents the Ashkenazi side of my family—it epitomizes it. Doesn't every Ashkenazi Jewish family have a sepia portrait of a man in full beard and immigrant clothes? In his long coat and puffed-up hat like a chef's toque, he props what looks to be a volume of Talmud on his knee. He died relatively young, in his late fifties, although he looks older than Methuselah. I covered his image with a sheet for good measure and superstitious protection, but sometimes I fantasized that La Tía and the rabbi walked out of their frames late at night and perhaps shared a cup of tea at my kitchen island. I liked to think they put aside their Ladino and Yiddish and conversed in a third tongue particular to my mixed ancestors; surely, language is not a barrier in the afterlife.

Also on display in my living room are the black and white photographs of my parents, where my father is a twenty-two-year-old ensign in the Navy and my mother is a nineteen-year-old beauty queen. My father is adrenaline skinny, with a thatch of chest hair poking out from under his shirt. My mother's tresses drape down her shoulder and back. Her lips are preternaturally dark. Her gaze is uncharacteristically serene; at that moment in time, she was *la mas linda en Havana.*

My mother is still alive, but she no longer bears any resemblance to that beauty queen. It's not so much that she has aged as that she has lived a life worn down by untold emotional turmoil and outwitting bad luck. For her, it's been an exhausting run. Her parents gave her the Hebrew name Mazal, luck, and for years it served her well—but now she inhabits the bad luck and ill humor she managed to defer for so long.

What do all these portraits have to say to me? What solace or wisdom might they offer? When I was young, my mother was furious that I looked so much like my father. It doesn't take much scrutinizing to see my face staring out from inside his. As I grow older, I worry that we share a genetic destiny; some days I wait for the Parkinson's tremors to start.

"There's no evidence that Parkinson's is hereditary," my husband tells me, and he, the scientist, would know.

"I want one of those DNA home kits," I announced one day. "The one that detects disease."

At the very least my ancestors could give me useful medical information. This could be their legacy to me.

"Do you really want to live your life knowing you're predisposed to an illness?" Ken asked.

"You said Parkinson's isn't hereditary!"

"But those tests can indicate markers for neurological disease," he explained. "And there are implications for your siblings if you go poking around in your genetics. Just be prepared; it's a Pandora's box. You have no idea what you'll find."

What else rattled around inside that Pandora's box? Were there other diseases and predispositions I hadn't anticipated?

As I Googled around, most of the horrible/wonderful stories that emerged were of people spitting their DNA samples into vials and coming up with phantom family members: the long-lost kind, the unexpected kind. Joyful reunions, but also unpleasant jolts of surprise. Which of these might be Ana?

As I began to contemplate my genetic history, Ana once again took up residence in my head like Rabbi Rosen's picture; or perhaps she had never left, but was merely stowed beneath a sheet in the attic of my mind. Ana, the Guatemalan mystery girl who showed up on our doorstep in the summer of 1972. Ana, the exchange student who just happened to choose West Hartford, who lived with another family but spent many of her waking hours with mine.

What was behind my sudden, desperate need to identify inherited diseases? Was it really all about Ana, suddenly springing forth from her mystical picture frame? Although I hadn't really understood back when she filled out our family booth at Howard Johnson's, over the years I'd come to regard her as my mother did—as my not totally unexpected half-sister. She had always been there, just beneath the surface, something I hadn't wanted to face but suddenly realized was possibly within reach.

Still, I wasn't sure how much I wanted to know. I started, like anyone does these days, by Googling. I steeled myself to jump into an Internet rabbit hole without an escape plan.

I typed in her name. Ana Hernandez was as common a name as you could imagine in Guatemala.

I tried social media. I tried "exchange student." It seemed hopeless.

The part of me that, for some reason, didn't want to locate her occasionally yielded and churned out another clue. Five years earlier, my brother had remembered the name of Ana's host family in West Hartford. I plugged their name, Gonzalez, directly into the search engine, and found hundreds of them—John knew this one had been a plastic surgeon in Hartford. That bit of information narrowed things right down to Arturo Gonzalez.

Once I had Arturo's original address and phone number, I could follow his moves over the years from Connecticut to the Cape to Rhode

Island. I could also find other names related to his on search sites. The Internet finally gifted me with the name of one of his daughters, Joanna—who, it turned out, lived near me in Boston. I found an address and phone number for her, and then I did what many a Google stalker has done: I walked away from it.

I wanted to know. I didn't want to know. For decades, Ana had been the unacknowledged daughter, the unclaimed sister. Was I ready to find her? To speak to her again? I guess not, because I left all the intelligence I had gathered on Post-its and scraps of notepaper. I ordered a DNA kit and left it, unopened, in the guest room, beneath a haphazard pile of books.

In occasional fits of paranoia over the next five years, I imagined that everyone but we, my father's children and his wife, knew my father's heart. Perhaps the Gonzalezes were in on his secret. They were an Argentinian family; maybe Dad had worked with Arturo in the CIA. Or, what if Ana were Joanna Gonzalez's sister instead of mine? Would that feel better or worse to me? Ana had bunked at their house, not mine—although my mother, wildly jealous, would never have allowed Ana to stay overnight under our roof. Contacting Joanna could end my mythic, grandiose, almost half-century relationship with Ana. The truth of her might be shocking or quotidian, but I feared that anything along that spectrum would be more than enough to destabilize the world I had built for myself, the one that had cushioned me from most of life's blows thus far.

And then, a miracle. Under the subject line "Look what I found," my sister emailed me a photo.

"I didn't even know I had this!" wrote Carol. "It was in the box of pictures I found at Asylum Avenue, mixed in with oldies, like the picture I found of Dad with Jack."

I nearly cried when I saw the photo of me and Ana, sitting together on Felipe's deck. Yes, Ana existed. I had not conjured her.

This time I looked up Arturo's daughter on Facebook and found we had a shared connection. "What is Joanna like?" I emailed our mutual friend, Erin.

Erin wrote back, "I used to attend church with her in Cambridge. She's lovely. I can introduce the two of you by email."

I thanked Erin and told her this was something I needed to do without a middle person. I wrote to Joanna that evening:

I remember your family hosted an exchange student one summer from Guatemala named Ana Hernandez. She was a frequent visitor to our house on Asylum Avenue. My siblings and I think there might be a familial connection. I know it may sound farfetched, but we believe she is our half-sister.

As soon as I hit the send button, I regretted it. What if this was the wrong Joanna Gonzalez and I had just spilled family secrets to a stranger?

It was late afternoon when the message took flight for Joanna's inbox. My heart beat quickly, my fingers twitchy on my smartphone. Refresh, refresh, refresh. I checked one more time before bed and there was this message:

Hi Judy:
It's great to hear Ana's name again! I adored her when I was a kid! I think she stayed with us for a year—but let me check with my sister. She may remember more.

I could hardly sleep. Joanna had added that she would love to talk. We eventually found a time—a Monday night. Making the phone call launched another week of searching, surmising and conjecture.

"Ana Hernandez," Joanna said on the phone, incredulous. "What a blast from the past!"

She said her mom, who had known Ana best, died a decade ago, and her father was now nearly a centenarian. "He's a voracious reader and very alert, but he doesn't remember much about her."

"I always wondered what brought her to our town in particular," I said. "Could she perhaps have been your family's au pair?"

"No, I remember she was studying, although I can't remember what."

"Did she come to you through an organization? An exchange program?"

"I can't recall. My mother taught at Wesleyan; maybe there was some connection there? Or it could have been a community thing."

"We had a lot of dinner guests from Latin America," I said, telling her about the potluck dinners with writers, poets, musicians. "There was some sort of pipeline in Hartford." I waited a beat to ask her: "Could your father have been in the CIA, too?"

"Absolutely not," Joanna said emphatically. I worried that I'd insulted her. "He was a socialist. He was arrested protesting the government when he was in medical school in Buenos Aires."

She and her sister had kept in touch with Ana for a while, "But honestly, she just disappeared from our lives. I don't have further information. My father and brother cleaned out the West Hartford house a long time ago, so those letters are gone."

Joanna's amnesia began to feel willful, intentional. She remained friendly, yet evasive. She admitted that she knew Ana had gotten married but didn't remember how she knew. "I had fantasies of going to Guatemala to visit her. One salient memory is that Ana told us the fields people worked in were sprayed and everyone was getting sick. It influenced my sister's choice to become an environmentalist."

"Did her family have a farm?"

"It seems that way, doesn't it?" Joanna said, laughing nervously, then blurting: "She must be about seventy years old," as if trying to caution me against disturbing the tranquility of Ana's golden years.

The conversation that had started so promisingly petered out. I finally broke up a stretch of stagnant quiet. "I guess Ana will remain a mystery," I said, hoping she would contradict me, that she would leap in to join my quest.

A pause. "I'll be in touch if I find anything," she said, her voice breaking. I knew I wouldn't hear from her again.

There was no way around it. I would have to go to Guatemala and look for Ana myself.

I don't know why I hadn't tried to do this earlier. Friends had asked me about the possibility, and somehow it hadn't registered. Or I hadn't let it. Every time I thought about tracking down Ana, my mind turned hazy or a migraine settled in.

I bought an airplane ticket to Guatemala City. I sent a deposit for an annual writing workshop held on Lake Atitlan, where an author I admired had a house, and was supportive and kind in her emails. She said she recognized the trip held significance for me in many ways, and she looked forward to introducing me around. Even if I never found Ana, I would be walking where she had walked, where my father had walked. Where perhaps my father had stowed away a second family.

I wanted to go. I didn't want to go. Did my body sense my hesitation? While visiting Adam who was on a fellowship in Spain a month before I was to leave for Lake Atitlan, a cobblestone on a quaint street rose up out of nowhere to meet me, and I landed hard enough so that I fractured my shoulder in three places. I boarded my flight the next day, but not before I was detained at the Madrid Airport. Why was I suddenly leaving the country? "Isn't it obvious?" I said, sitting in a wheelchair, my arm in a complicated sling. The pain was talking, and I spoke Spanish, which somehow made me more suspicious.

"Your accent is good," said the immigration officer.

"My mother is from Cuba."

"Beautiful country," he said. Suddenly, all was forgiven, and I was wheeled onto the airplane ten minutes before it took off. Half of the people on board were masked, and I wondered if I should be masked too. I flew home in a haze of opioids. My seatmate—a sweet college student sent home by his study abroad program—opened my soda can for me. He said my groaning didn't bother him. An hour later, he moved seats.

Two weeks later, we were officially in a pandemic, and even if I had wanted to, I could not go to Guatemala, not then or for the foreseeable future. The author, who had been so solicitous regarding my personal journey, did not refund any part of the hefty tuition she charged for the workshop.

Locked down at home, locked out of Guatemala, stalled on the Internet, I fished out the DNA kit from five years ago. Rather than a Pandora's box I visualized it as a black box, the kind recovered in airplane crashes that held the mysteries of a tragedy in the making. Finding Ana would be more than genetic confirmation; it would be the unraveling of a story tightly coiled in my heart. Did Dad create an entire life, another family, during his time in Guatemala? It was something the spy in white gloves would have done. It was something my mother had always been certain he'd done. "One day, there will be a knock at the door . . ."

The DNA kit had long expired.

I convinced myself that it was a long shot, anyway. A few years ago, there were eight million people in the various DNA databases. What were the chances I'd find Ana?

But now, long after my kit had expired, there were thirty-five million in that database. Not such a long shot as I had feared, or hoped.

Not a problem, said the 23andMe representative when I explained about my hesitance and the expiration date. The company would send me a new one, free of charge.

It was time to spit into the vial. It was time to wade in the vast gene pool to which my home DNA kit contributed. But after tearing the plastic off the packaging, I froze. What if I wasn't who I thought I was? My mind went to alarming, if improbable, places. What if I were linked to someone like the Golden State Killer, who was found only because of an unsuspecting family member's dabbling in DNA? We'd not only be a family with a spy who went rogue and settled down with an adding machine, but a family with a hardcore criminal floating in our genetic stew.

My mouth was dry. Anna, who worked at Children's Hospital, was an expert at getting three-year-olds to produce spittle, so she went to work on me.

"Hey, maybe we're related to Michael Bolton the singer!" she said. The singer's people also had settled in New Haven, and their last name was originally Bolotin, like mine. But Anna's attempts to cheer me into spitting didn't work.

"You can do this, Mom," she said gently. "Think of something yummy."

I wanted to know. I didn't want to know. Curiosity killed the cat. But a cat has nine lives and probably many cousins. At the very least, I contained the multitudes from which Walt Whitman spun poetry.

The findings from these kits can upend a life. I am Judy Bolton, daughter of Harold and Matilde, related to the Duke of Albuquerque, who lived in fifteenth century Spain. Am I not?

It took a good half-hour of Anna's coaxing for me to produce an adequate sample. I sealed the vial, packed it up and mailed it, squeezing my eyes shut as I dropped it into the box. My spittle went off to a DNA factory where it would join thousands, if not thousands of thousands, of gallons of samples. I had read about a company selling 1.5 million home genetic kits over one long holiday weekend in 2017; the author estimated it amounted to 2,000 gallons of spit, enough to fill an average above-ground swimming pool, the kind I almost drowned in at Felipe's house. Such a pool would contain the genetic history of every person in a city the size of Philadelphia.

A few weeks later, 23andMe sent various hyperlinks to my results. When I didn't immediately click through to my DNA reports, my reluctance seemed to concern the company. I received several email messages nudging me to open my test results and take a look. After a week of their entreaties, I decided to start with the safest link of all, one that was standard for everyone as part of the results but that probably would yield no information whatsoever, what they called the Neanderthal Report. I figured I could gradually work up to other, more normal ancestry choices, like "European." After all, I am not a cavewoman; I descend from royalty.

I clicked on the "safe" report and, horrified, saw that I had ten percent more Neanderthal DNA than the average 23andMe consumer. I was prehistoric! At least, some of my DNA was. I waited a few more days to calm down from this unwelcome information before clicking through the other links.

I tried the ancestry composition link and found another bell I could not unring—not only was I prehistoric, I was just barely over sixty percent Ashkenazi Jewish and almost fifteen percent Southern European.

No sign of the Duke of Albuquerque, and certainly no sign of Ana. To the contrary, my spit revealed I was only one-and-a-half percent Spanish—hardly Spanish at all! Whereas I was nine percent Italian, with slivers of the Middle East and Africa. I didn't recognize any of the names of the relatives dangling from the family tree that 23andMe had planted for me. I noticed, though, that I distantly matched people with Latino surnames. I was everything and nothing. Undefined. My narrative was now open to full-on speculation. I was dizzy with the possibilities of who I was or, more accurately, who I thought I was.

Or wasn't.

Disoriented and disappointed, I decided to upload my DNA results onto another site with the hope of gaining more clarity. MyHeritage also confirmed that I am only a little over sixty percent Ashkenazi, but promoted me to twenty-two percent Sephardic. The numbers still didn't compute. To the best of anyone's knowledge, my mother was a full Sephardic Jew, with parents from established Sephardic families in Turkey and Greece. I looked up my DNA matches and recognized some distant relatives, a couple of whom I had even met. There was also a sprinkling of "Albukreks," Rosens, and Behars. For a moment, these results seemed more credible. Yet I still felt disconnected to the world at large. Was my family smaller than average? Or maybe it was just a family in which no one had thus far been willing to spit into a vial. Blood, in this case, was thicker than DNA.

I began to think a laboratory technician might have confused my DNA with someone else's. This was not the right swimming pool. Even more distressing was that I flashed back to the little girl I was when my mother told me in her white-hot anger that I was switched at birth in the hospital. "I'm not your mother," she said, and I cried myself into panic. Now, my adult panic sat in my belly, further excavating the deep pit already there.

During this DNA confusion, two dreams seemed to confirm my instinct to retreat from biology and personal history. In one, my father gives me the same order again to "Leave this alone." He is driving me in the '65 Malibu, his hands gripping a wheel large enough to steer a boat, maybe his ship during the war. Although I am grown, a half-size violin case sits across my lap as if I am on my way to another futile lesson—a reminder that I will never please my music-loving father.

In the second dream, Ana takes me down dark corridors lined with funhouse mirrors, where I see distorted images of us—our father's head atop our bodies, making us new-fangled beasts of our own mythology. What was the mangled DNA of these creatures?

I could not bear to examine the DNA findings any further. A friend gently pressed me to consult an interpreter, someone who could parse the results on my behalf. She put me in touch with Diane, an enthusiastic amateur genealogist. I told Diane I didn't know a haplogroup from a chromosome and that I had begun this experiment with only one clear goal: to find my father's Guatemalan daughter.

Diane was cheerful and smart and patient—a winning combination for moody, scattered me. She sent detailed instructions on how to understand the reports that represented chaos to me. My acute anxiety blurred any comprehension I could have mustered. Diane eventually went ahead and interpreted the entire family tree, and came back with a sober assessment: "I had hoped to find Ana, but you have to understand, people in Latin America tend not to take these tests."

Ana was not in the spittle swimming pool with me. At least, as Diane corrected me, the results were inconclusive.

I looked again at the photo of me and Ana, trying to dream myself back into that time, trying to see if I had left any clues behind. I looked to be about eleven years old. I had loved the blouse I was wearing—green with white Swiss dots. I wore it often. I show some hint of a chest. I am looking at Ana as she looks straight into the camera—a sweet smile, gesturing with her right hand. Seventy years old now? Impossible. Ana is forever young. Forever sweet. I think of the party where Dad ferried Carol around like a precious doll, where I hear his laughter again as he says of Ana and Carol, "They could be sisters."

"I would have loved to have an older sister," I tell a friend.

"Are you sure?" she asks.

Here was the beating heart of my question: Did my father love Ana more than he loved me? She was the daughter of his youth and passion.

When I came along in the middle of his life, I tied him to my mother and me forever. Had he wanted me? Had he resented me?

Did he hate me?

Sarah, the medium who lobbed guesses rather than revelations, during our awkward session had held up four fingers to represent my father's four children, not three. Ana toppled me from my special place as first-born. She bundled Carol and me together in the middle of the brood.

Carol and Ana were my father's clear favorites. And why not? At Dad's beloved Yale Bowl games, Carol was his cheerleader, screaming, "Rough the kicker!" Had Ana been here, I picture her whistling between her fingers like Grandpa Bolton did every time Yale scored. Whereas I was the daughter who worried the navy blue rabbit's foot Dad bought me for luck, and buried my nose in a book during exciting plays and marching band antics. He eventually gave up on me and stopped taking me to the Bowl.

According to Sarah, my father wanted me to "let sleeping dogs lie." Was that what he was thinking when he issued the shaky Parkinsonian order for me to burn his letter that summer when I lived at the Y? At first blush, I obeyed him because I was the faithful daughter. But there was something more—I believed I could garner his affection if I did not expose the secret he had buried so assiduously. I believed he would love me more if I faithfully protected him. But he hated weakness, and in 1985 I was not yet bold enough to contradict him, a man who overthrew foreign governments before dinnertime. My father wanted to change history. As for me, despite my curiosity, my snooping, I was like the adoptee who doesn't want to find her family of origin. Is that what Judy Bolton, Girl Detective, had become? The one who preferred to leave the black box closed?

A move to confirm Ana's paternity might lay something to rest for me, but it would betray my father's *trastiendas* and unleash the same burning lava of emotions in my mother that had rumbled so close to the surface for the decades we lived at 1735 Asylum. I could feel the tremors starting again, her ruinous fury from which I shrank until I disappeared inside myself, a vanishing act that was not magic, but an embodiment of what the Kabbalists called *tsimtsum*—contracting as God did at the beginning of time to make room for the creation of the world. Just before God went into exile, he left behind vessels he filled with his divine light. But the vessels could not contain God's holy illumination, and they exploded, scattering shards of that potent light everywhere. Those shards multiplied and now we spend time searching for them with no end. This leaves us with the reality that we cannot fix what is broken. And just as this heartbreaking fact marks the beginning of trauma in the world, I am similarly bereft. How can I continue to search for a woman for whom there is not enough room in my soul?

I thought it would be overwhelming to see Ana's image again after all these years, but what struck me about the photo Carol had unearthed was how alone I was in the world. I did not smile at the camera. I never smiled in those days.

As I study the photo, I stared at my chest again—hints of woman-hood to come—and my eyes fill with tears. I'm surprised to find myself going back in time, back to the '65 Chevy Malibu. My father is driving me to a violin lesson, and I am wearing the stretchy purple shirt in which I felt so pretty. The shirt perfectly matches my pink and purple plaid culottes. Although I am almost thirteen, I am not allowed to shave my legs yet, so I cover my hairiness with white knee socks.

My father and I are uncomfortably quiet. He has not set off on his familiar harangue about my mother or her germophobic relatives who don't open windows even in summer. But something is coming. We pass a girl on a bicycle and he turns to take a second look at her. The girl is what my mother would call a *tetona*. She is busty, and even though she is seated on her bike, I know she is curvy in a way that I cannot at that moment imagine I will ever be.

"That's a pretty girl," my father remarks. He goes silent for a beat. "When are you going to finally look like a woman?"

I knew then and there in the Malibu that I would never have a turn at being *la mas linda della familia*. I was not Spanish gorgeous like Carol. I was not classically beautiful like my mother when she stepped out with my father on a Saturday night. I did not have my father's favor like Ana.

My father never looked at me the way he looked at Ana or, for those few cringing moments, the stranger on the bicycle.

It came over me anew: the humiliation in the Malibu, the sadness that no one had noticed the girl in the picture with the green shirt. No one cared to find out why she never smiled. No one cherished her all those years ago.

I come back to the present where I am safe and loved.

I have come to understand that the biology of emotions is too nuanced for any DNA kit to detect. No amount of spitting into a vial can reveal the pure truth of my essence. Nor is tracing my DNA the making of an accident scene. There is no black box of unintelligible static that will uncover the mystery of Ana. I know what I know. Ana was once in our lives, however briefly, and she might be my half-sister. But, to stop another tsimtsum, I leave these matters where they are. I do not wish to withdraw again from a world I have purposefully and lovingly built.

CHAPTER 21

Beharismo

A single waxy candle atop a large piece of cheesecake casts a flickering glow, highlighting the childish joy on my mother's face. I sang happy birthday to her, along with John, both of us stumbling over the three syllables of Ma-til-de. Mom was turning seventy-three and had asked the befuddled servers if she looked her age; they didn't know what to say. She looked more than her age.

By 2009, my mother's feral life had caught up with her, overtaken her. She had perfected a magnificent and complicated dance in which she drew in the people she needed to help her survive. It was an encompassing group dance with Mom in the center, as always, right hand on her stomach and left hand in the air, dancing by herself. Lines were deeply etched in her powdered and rouged skin. Her black wavy hair had gone gray. Anyone could see that she had once been a beautiful woman—but that was long ago, back when she was the self-proclaimed Duchess of Albuquerque.

"Mom, you are eternal," I told her. What I meant to say was that there was no end to her. She would live forever—"through a nuclear winter," according to Carol.

With just misery for company, my mother was lonely. No one in her extended family had contacted Matilde *la peleona*—the fighter—in years. With each passing birthday her world shrank, just as it had once been limited to stops along the Asylum Avenue bus line. She still boarded the

Peter Pan Bus to Boston to see her grandchildren, but only if it was a straight shot, not requiring her to change buses in Springfield.

No one telephoned her anymore. "The screaming is too much for me," her cousin Rafael told me when I sought him out in Miami. Carol and I had always called him the family icon, known for his devotion to his mother, La Tiá Rashél. At eleven years old, Rafael sold newspapers and peddled rags in Havana to support his mother—a thin, sad woman, scarred by childhood smallpox and afflicted with loneliness and migraines. She never touched another man after her husband left her.

"What does my mother scream about?" I asked Rafael.

"You, your father's illness, her terrible mazal. She screams and screams as if it's my fault that my luck is good. *Me entiendes?*"

Yes, I understood perfectly.

"She has *Beharismo*," said Rafael. What he meant to say is that the Behars—Abuela's clan—was cursed. Like an Italian family I once read about that had suffered for generations from fatal familial insomnia, the Behars, originally from Saranta Ekklisies in Greece, succumbed in every generation to fatal familial unhappiness.

"Let me tell you your mother's problem," he said. *"Beharismo, chica. No hay otra explicacíon."* There was no other explanation.

Beharismo waxed and waned as my mother took up her life story yet again during her birthday lunch. She went all the way back to her first winter in the United States. "The cold almost killed me," she said, making no mention this time of Manuel, writing him out of the current permutation of the story. "I went back to Cuba the next year, but there was nothing for me there."

She saw Castro's name painted on every wall. His takeover was imminent. "Castro was making so much noise in the Sierra Maestra Mountains you could hear him all the way in Havana," my mother said. "Cuba was dangerous. My father sent me back to his cousins in Brooklyn."

I exchanged looks with John, who was as interested in our family history as I was. He had been encouraging me to dig for Dad's story. We both hoped that our mother would let slip inadvertent clues about Dad and the CIA that would help us in our investigation, although we doubted that he would have entrusted his explosive wife with such classified information about himself or the country he loved.

John and I had recently discussed how strange it was that Abuelo, who barely let his daughter out of the house in Havana, allowed her to go the United States on her own. It was as if she were a pallet of goods to be moved across the border. My brother excused himself from the table and went outside to text me.

"Ask her to tell you about her old man and the 10K," he wrote.

The ten thousand dollars had to do with the drama of our family's escape from Cuba. We wanted a working timeline of events, but Mom's stream-of-consciousness thinking was foiling our attempts. These stories of hers have always been hard to follow, let alone believe; yet, they have always been impossible to leave alone. They were consistent enough to make us think they held some truth. John and I were looking to land at the intersection where our father's intentions toward our mother crossed over with his CIA mission. It was also the time when the Cuban Revolution came to Callé Mercéd 20, in the fall of 1960.

My parents had finally married and Mom was immediately pregnant with me. She told the story of how she was cleaning up one day and her big belly knocked over Dad's tanning lamp. "Your father sat under that lamp in the middle of the winter to look as dark as a *negrito*." Early on in investigating Dad's CIA career, my brother surmised that Dad sat under that lamp so he could match the skin tone of the average Guatemalan, "so he wouldn't stand out."

John waited for my return text.

I dutifully asked my mother, "Tell me again about the ten thousand dollars."

She was only too happy to talk about the time Abuelo burned ten thousand American dollars in a hurry after the head of the neighborhood watch pointed him out as antirevolutionary.

"Those *hijos de mala madres* were suspicious of your abuelo because I was married to an American," she said. "Castro wanted me to go back and serve the revolution. I got a telegram telling me exactly that when we lived in East Hartford."

I'd heard the story for as long as I could remember, but for the first time wondered why the Castro government would bother to track down my mother in Connecticut. It didn't seem like a good use of time for a burgeoning regime.

I steered my mother back on course. "Abuelo? The money?"

"He burned ten thousand dollars in the bathtub."

"Where was the money before he burned it?"

"In the house. He didn't trust banks."

That part I believed. My grandfather had alluded to it, as had Aunt Reina. They were the under-the-mattress kind of savers.

"Why didn't he send the money with you to the United States?"

"*Ay. No se.* I don't know, he should have. Too many questions, Judy Bolton. You've been a *chismosa* since the day you were born."

"I'm not nosy, I'm curious," I argued. "I'm the family historian."

My phone vibrated; it was John again. I tried a different tack with my mother.

"How did Abuelo save so much money on a fabric salesman's salary?" I asked. "You told me you sent money back to Cuba while you were working in New York in the early days. How did he come to have all that money in US dollars?"

"*No mas,*" she said, shrill. "This is an Inquisition. I want a lawyer."

"Your son is a lawyer."

"John is not on my side. He asks too many questions, too."

I glanced down at John's latest text. "Don't you see what's going on?" he wrote. "Her old man was a patsy. Someone like the CIA paid him to send his beautiful daughter to the United States. They promised him they'd get her a husband."

"Excuse me a moment," I said to my mom, and texted back: "You're approaching her level of crazy."

"Think about it. A guy like Abuelo who just eked out a living could never save that kind of money."

I looked up at my mother. "Tell me one more thing," I said. "Why did your strict father, a man who barely let you out of the house, allow you to go to the United States all by yourself?"

"I told you, there was no future in Cuba," she said.

"Why didn't he send your sister with you? You and Aunt Reina could have taken care of each other."

"Reina was engaged to Enrique."

"Did he send you alone so you could find a husband here?"

My mother looked heavenward. "*Ay Dio de la zedakades*, tell her to stop." But I couldn't stop.

"Isn't it true that in a Sephardic house the older daughter has to marry before the younger one is allowed?"

My mother lost patience. "Where's John?" she demanded. "Why is he away so long?"

"I'll text him," I said, and wrote to him: "You might be onto something after all."

"Damn right," John muttered to me when he returned to the table. "Damn right."

As soon as we dropped my mother off at home, John and I got to work on our theory at a Starbucks.

"Her old man sold her off for 10K," said John. "It's obvious the CIA bought his silence. How else do you explain a strict father sending his twenty-two-year-old daughter to the United States alone?"

"They had plenty of material for a cover story," I agreed. "She was difficult and strong-willed and, let's face it, unpopular in the family; all that was a plus. It makes the cover story plausible. From Mom's point of view, 'girl comes to America for a better life.' From her father's point of view, he sends away a troubled daughter. It clicks."

"The question is, could Abuelo be trusted to be a de facto spy?" asked John.

"The CIA has done worse," I said. "Although it seems like a lot of energy to expend on getting one man placed in Havana."

"We don't know how key Dad was to the operation."

"We don't know if there was an operation."

At the end of the birthday lunch, my mother had blown out her candle and made a wish as if she were a child. "Happy birthday to me," she said, clapping her hands.

John and I knew extracting any noteworthy information from her would be hopeless. She couldn't possibly know Dad's secret, and we would never tell her.

CHAPTER 22

1735 Asylum Avenue

The house at 1735 Asylum Avenue and I crept deeply into middle age.

Half a century after my parents moved into the house, it wasn't holding up well and neither was I. I took several pills a day for high blood pressure, cholesterol, anxiety and depression, and none of those medications did me any good as Carol, John, and I cleaned out the old place. Dad had been dead for over a decade and it was time to move my mother into assisted living. To keep the job from steamrolling us, we each claimed a room to empty.

Those last years at 1735 Asylum, we choked on our ongoing agitation as much as on the years of dust that had accumulated. We begged, fought, and threatened our mother in hopes of getting her to see it was time to leave. When we finally cleared the place from top to bottom, my mother was in a rehab facility after stomach surgery and had finally, grudgingly, consented to selling the house. Her last night at 1735 Asylum had been two months earlier when she called me in a panic that she had been dizzy and nauseated for days. From my home in Boston I called a Hartford ambulance, and after so many false alarms, this time she went to the hospital.

"I brought these," said my sister, holding up a box of latex gloves as we worked together. These were the gloves typically worn by a medical person to take blood or administer a shot. Dad's aides snapped them on to toilet him or wipe his drool. Now it was our turn to wear them in a house where a family of raccoons recently lived in the chimney, and we had to pick through the mouse droppings in the kitchen. We wore masks to avoid inhaling mold and dust. We must have looked like mad surgeons or germophobic bank robbers.

For years I dreamed of the day when a wrecking ball would smash into 1735 Asylum. I would take pictures upon the first impact. I would cheer. I would cry. I would watch the house die so I could dance around its open grave. But that's not what happened. The house went to a builder who intended to take it down to the studs, to renovate everything, including the unhappiness embedded in its walls. We cut a deal with him to dispose of anything we left behind. This meant abandoning the green-swirled sofa with old circulars under its cushions. The hi-fi missing the *a* in Magnavox. The dining table with its warped leaves, beneath which I had sat as a little girl when my parents alternately entertained and fought their way through another year of marriage. The chipped lamp of the cow jumping over the moon that dimly lit the bedroom I had shared with my sister.

As my siblings and I waded through the wreckage of 1735, we were mindful of looking for paperwork, pictures, or letters that proved or even suggested that Dad had been in the CIA. I searched for the scallop-edged photograph of Dad in Guatemala. I looked for old check registers and date books that might have placed him out of the country, particularly during the time we were in Miami. In a house full of old stuff, these items were strangely missing among junk that no longer mattered. Perhaps what I was looking for was not there because the house had not been kept up after the early 1980s. My mother had once been fastidious about tidying the place and throwing out stuff she no longer needed. I would have to continue imagining my way into the past.

I volunteered to go through everything in my old stomping ground—the master bedroom. I needed to be alone one last time with the detritus of my parents' lives.

The first thing I came upon was my master's degree thesis. The collection of short stories was the work of a young writer—heavily autobiographical material studded with awkward observations about my father. The title story alone, "The Ninety-Day Wonder," reflects how long I'd had my obsession with my father's tamped-down, secretive biography. "Here is what I think I know about him," the story began. "My aunt said that when he came back from the war, he was wide-eyed. Not a blink. Not a current of life going through him. She said it happened to men stationed in the South Pacific. But I suspect that he missed expansiveness, that he missed blue and white. He missed the steel gray water chopped in increments."

Over time, I came to understand how much my father did miss the expansiveness of the Pacific Ocean. Until the day he died, he was wide-eyed from staring at the horizon during his five years of service. He had been a young officer and, for better or worse, a Ninety-Day Wonder—a newbie—who exerted himself as if treading water, learning the basic facts about what it took to get by as a naval officer. In that first story, I hurriedly moved on to cover Dad's stint in South America. "Of his time in Guatemala, my father says this and only this: 'What a beautiful paradise and what beautiful people.' . . . My mother's long-standing accusation is that he married down there and ditched his [Guatemalan] wife and child." Ana. I had always suspected she was his daughter.

My father had bookmarked the title story. Maybe he also lingered over the dedication to my mother and him. Maybe he anticipated these stories as his legacy, as yet another version of a Kaddish. But here is what I definitely knew from rereading my thesis: I never stopped investigating his aura of mystery and my mother's Cubana-ness.

By the time we sold 1735 Asylum Avenue in 2012, the house bore only faint traces of my father's existence. His chairlift had scarred the wall leading upstairs. The tire marks of his wheelchair streaked the hallway's pale beige carpeting. I found a dusty case of Earth's Best baby food still in the cupboard from when it was the only food he could swallow.

"How old is your baby now?" the manager at Whole Foods once asked me when I regularly bought my father cases of Earth's Best.

"Eighty-three," I replied.

My mother's imprint on the house, however, was heavy. Years of hoarding had left her barricaded behind unopened boxes of shoes and unworn piles of clothing she had ordered from the Home Shopping Network. High school Spanish tests that she administered in the '70s and '80s still cluttered her world, as did stacks of old greeting cards. She had saved our disintegrating baby clothes along with my prom gown and the dress I wore to my high school graduation.

Maybe it was just a sign of old age—an unkempt house filled with markers of the helter skelter chronology of her life. Or maybe it was her bulwark against the time when she'd have to leave.

When my father died, the house was still habitable. But then the heater broke down and the sump pump—what Dad always lectured was crucial to the upkeep of a house—wasn't up to the task of keeping the basement dry. Weeds shot through the cracks in the driveway. The shrubs demarcating the backyard were overgrown. Bird droppings streaked the window air conditioners, which wheezed dramatically in the summer humidity.

My mother's gait had become halting, between the bad knees and the eroding will to go anywhere. Yet she refused to use a cane, and we lived in fear that she would fall and break a hip, or worse. She refused to consider moving to Boston to be closer to Carol and me. Hartford was the home she had made with my father and the place where she knew the bus lines, the television channels, and the best supermarket for tuna salad.

Carol suggested that we team up to clean the living room. To start, we had to work around a water-damaged piano, two coffee tables that my mother had somehow accumulated for a space that fit one, and the large white sofa with green swirls. I half expected, half wished, to see my father sitting at the end of the sofa, his regular perch after dinner, where he read beneath a circle of light. He was all concentration and intelligence when he had his nose in a book.

Twenty years before this final cleaning stint at 1735 Asylum Avenue, we had purged his thick library of Michener and Wouk novels from a basement full of mold and mouse droppings. Slumped in his recliner in the den, Dad silently watched us carry his memories to a dumpster in the driveway.

"*Ladrones*," thieves, my mother accused us as we removed our college textbooks, now waterlogged. My mother's novels by Cervantes and

Miguel de Unamuno that came from Spain were also soaked. When she could take no more of this purging, she dialed the police. "I'm being robbed," she screamed.

From the beginning of my father's decline, the West Hartford police and fire departments had come to know my mother even better than they had when they answered domestic calls at our address decades earlier. A significant number of the new crop of officers and firefighters had been her students at Northwest Catholic, and they looked out for her. She called when my father fell out of bed or she locked herself out of the house, both with increasing frequency. We called them, too, if Mom didn't answer the phone late at night.

One of the two policemen who arrived to arrest us for the massive housecleaning we were doing that day had flunked my mother's Spanish Two class. "You got old," she said when she saw him.

"That's better than what you told me last time," he replied with a laugh. Turning to us, he said, "She told me I was the stupidest kid in her class."

"I want these two *putas* off my property and in jail," my mother said referring to Carol and me.

"Mrs. Bolton, you don't really want me to arrest your daughters, do you?" asked her former student.

"I don't care what happens to them! I'll get a restraining order!"

"Okay, I can do that for you," he said, winking at Carol and me. His partner seemed to have little patience for the unfolding fiasco.

My mother turned around to start up the stairs. Despite her slow and creaking pace, Carol and I instantly knew that she was headed for the bathroom to grab my father's silver razor and threaten to slash her wrists. We had been down this road before. We also knew that the razor would be hovering above her arm until we rushed in and pleaded with her to stop. Once we made the second officer aware of the scene my mother was about to set up, she took the stairs two at a time and knocked on the bathroom door. She needn't have bothered; my mother never locked the door during one of these dramas. She wanted someone to find her in mid-action.

"Jesus, she's gonna kill herself!" said the panicked policewoman.

The ex-student suggested that we commit her involuntarily. "I'm sorry," the female officer said, "but I'll have to call an ambulance." But the ex-student had been through this before, too. He said, "She's just being dramatic."

No matter how we tried to convince the other officer, it looked like my mother was finally caught. Outside of the family, we never told a soul about the times she poised a steak knife to plunge into her belly or threatened to slit her wrists. But my mother was not the problem. If we committed her, what would we do about Dad? He was barely mobile by his mid-seventies. My mother was in charge of his hodgepodge care. Our lives—living on a corner lot in a pricey suburb, my parents' glossy Saturday night appearances, the children scrubbed to shine and show off—had all been *pegado con chicle*, stuck together with the same sticky gum that kept my parents together. The same gum that superficially kept us intact. Maybe this was the day the *chicle* lost its glue. Or maybe it was our version of *kintsugi,* the Japanese philosophy of embracing the flawed or imperfect. This means valuing an object even if it breaks. It's a rationalization for keeping an object even if it has shattered. The cracks and repairs are distinguished in gold. Maybe that's what we were when we assembled as a family—beautiful flawed objects that continued to survive despite our damage.

By the time the ambulance arrived, my mother was properly dressed for company. She had once again decided to postpone suicide for another day.

"She's a danger to herself," said the woman cop.

"Never to herself," I muttered under my breath.

"I'm not going anywhere," my mother said, close to a tantrum. "I feel fine. It's these two who are the *locas.*" She pointed to Carol and me. She told the EMTs that we were dismantling her home, ruining her life. Given those circumstances, anyone would naturally be upset. Carol and I knew that to press on with getting her in front of a psychiatrist was futile.

"Don't forget about my restraining order," she said to her former student as everyone was leaving, including the EMTs. "I hope it's not as hard for you to remember as stem-changing verbs."

He turned around. "Nothing," he said, "is as hard as conjugating those damn stem-changing verbs."

On that last day in the house, I asked Carol if she would miss the place. "Too much has happened here," she said. I knew what she meant. Our parents had papered the place with emotions that ranged from my mother's plate-throwing mania to my father's closet-drinking depression.

There had also been moments of love. My parents' age difference—a gulf, a bay, maybe the Bay of Pigs between them—vanished as they danced a smoked, stoked cha-cha at one of their hi-fi-blasting parties. People heard about their soirees through word of mouth at the Cuban social club: Meet at Harold and Matilde's on Asylum Avenue with a dish in hand—picadillo or paella! The blue noir of cigarette smoke, the stink of beer, and the danger of rum filled the house at those Saturday night potlucks when my mother willed herself to forget that the food people brought was not kosher.

For all the ambivalence I had about 1735 Asylum, selling it unmoored me. I felt adrift without the ancestral home and without my father the lieutenant commander there to guide me. All the years I had lived in New York City, Asylum Avenue was the only address printed on my driver's license. It was only reluctantly that we abandoned the phone number we'd had for half a century. The black rotary phone on which it rang was still rented from the phone company.

My mother swore that she would stay at 1735 Asylum until death did part her from that crumbling house. She screamed that she wanted to be buried *seis pies*—six feet under—in the backyard, even though there was a double plot, half of it already occupied by my father, waiting for her at Beth Israel Cemetery in Avon, Connecticut. The neighbors must have thought us to be the most negligent children in the world as they watched our limping mother haul garbage pails to the curb on Sunday nights, or noticed that her sidewalk remained unshoveled for days after a snowstorm. She lied to us and said that her lawn man did snow removal. She lied to us that she had a lawn man.

Giving up this house was anathema to my mother, who had not seen her home on Callé Mercéd in Old Havana since 1959. From the outside, it looked as if my siblings and I had forced her into another exile. Like my grandparents, who eventually walked away from decades of silver and jewelry and dishes, we shut the door on the house in West Hartford that was full of worn furniture, chipped glasses, and tattered clothes.

In the end, we too had gone into exile.

My mother needed a permanent place to live, and I was back at my old Catholic high school—The Mount—on a reconnaissance mission. Although the Mount had been through a few incarnations since I graduated, and was an official historic landmark, its exterior mandated for preservation in perpetuity, for the past decade it had also been an assisted living residence, named Hamilton Heights after the school's address. I had heard that they gave Mount alumnae impromptu tours, so on one of my trips back to West Hartford I decided to look into it as a possible place for my mother to live.

It was disorienting to use the front entrance, something strictly prohibited when I was a student. Tracy, the head of admissions, met me in the foyer and greeted me with the story of an older Mount graduate who came to see Hamilton Heights as a potential resident, and was so awash in memories of nuns rapping her knuckles with rulers that she refused to get out of the car.

I graduated as salutatorian in 1978—the last class to receive Mount diplomas, as the school had grown cavernous in an era of declining enrollment, making it too expensive to run. Tracy was curious as to why the reception area we were standing in was called "The Pope's Room."

"They had a chair here where Pope Pius XII actually sat when he visited one time," I explained.

"A Pope was *here*?" asked Tracy, incredulous.

I knew all about that chair. Before I graduated, I pulled off an act of rebellion: I had to claim the one thing that the nuns held so precious. I had to sit in the Pope's Chair.

On a dreary winter afternoon my senior year, I sneaked into that first-floor parlor. I was in my navy blue blazer and skirt, and knee-socked according to the Mount's dress code, to do the most defiant thing a Jewish girl could do at that school: I sat in a chair once occupied by Pope Pius XII.

The year before, the timid Spanish teacher Miss Welch had inducted me into the National Honor Society in that once-gracious parlor. The chair, in the center of the room, had a plush dark red seat and an austere mahogany wood back. Fancy braided ropes cordoned it off. Unlike the other furniture in the room, someone frequently dusted it.

The gold plaque on the chair said the Pope had sat there in 1953, a one-off event. I didn't know when I sat in the chair about Pius's immoral silence during the Holocaust, only that I was a Jew doing something provocative, even blasphemous. My bravado felt exciting, dangerous. I grabbed the arms of the chair, sweaty-palmed and shaky-kneed, until Pauline, my lookout, saw the rosy-cheeked principal, Sister Patricia, round the corner. Pauline cued me and I bolted up and hid behind the heavy curtain until it was safe to step out.

The Mount, reinvented as Hamilton Heights, was now decorated in false cheer. Tracy said the residents thought Hamilton Heights was haunted. She said that people saw doorknobs suddenly jiggle, windows slam shut, elevators randomly open and close. Tracy and I worked our way from the top of the building where the nuns once lived down to the basement cafeteria. The nuns' quarters and classrooms were now small apartments. The model apartment I saw encompassed the rooms where I'd had English and Spanish classes. The gym was now the Alzheimer's unit. The chapel was a meeting room—its stained-glass windows, representing the Twelve Stations of the Cross, still intact. I remembered that my only foray into mass had been to receive my class ring, with Brenda Callahan hissing behind me: "Kneel, little Jew. You killed our Lord and you have to pay!" It was the only anti-Semitism I experienced at the Mount. I had not realized until then that I was powerful enough to kill someone's god.

My mother couldn't bear the idea of living at the revamped Mount Saint Joseph Academy. She couldn't imagine living anywhere but 1735

Asylum Avenue, yet she eventually and grudgingly moved up the road to another assisted living apartment house.

Although the builder promised that everything left behind in our old house—furniture, old clothing, cracked dishes—would be quickly, efficiently, and discreetly disposed of, there were raids on the house. Its furnishings languished in the front and back yards. People came in pick-up trucks, U-hauls, and minivans to take away my parents' bedroom set, the threadbare sofa from the den, and my father's recliner. One of my mother's aides had been on the scene and said that strangers fought over the living and dining room sets.

"It felt like looting," said the aide. "They even took the scrappiest clothes. If I'd known this was going to happen, I would have taken the dining room table before it was out there for the world to grab."

I hoped that my bedroom set went to a little girl who would feel like a princess despite the chips on the white-and-gold etched headboard.

CHAPTER 23

La Callé Mercéd

Havana was once a sexy, rum-soaked playground for spies and the Mafia alike until Castro came down from the Sierra Maestra Mountains and marched into the city on New Year's Day 1959. Over a half-century later, I walked those same streets where my mother had dreamed of a wealthy life in America.

I strolled around Havana, taking in its gorgeous ruins. Cuba was an aging beauty queen that rose above decades of neglect and poverty, translucent with pastel colors and prism-like light.

There was a hunger in the street for things that I, as an American visitor, might be able to offer the people of Havana. The requests were humble, children asking for *caramelitos* and *plumas*—candies and pens. I gave them some pens that wrote in purple ink from a frilly Boston nail salon. The women in a state-run pharmacy flagged me down to ask if I had any medicine in my purse. The cab driver who took me to the University of Havana asked if I had any antacids or aspirin I could spare; his wife suffered from *migrañas*.

"There is nothing here," he said, gesturing widely at Cuba itself. "Look at this old Lada that I drive; every morning I pray it will start. *Estoy aburrido de esta vida.*" He was sick and tired of his life.

His was a lassitude mixed with the same Cuban melancholia my mother had. She too was *aburrida* with the life she led in America. She wanted to go back in time to a Cuba of warmth and ocean and Purim balls, of a lavishness she could almost touch. I told the driver how much my mother missed Cuba, and he bristled. "What is there to miss here anymore? Tell your mother not to come home. It's not the Havana she remembers."

He took me to the University of Havana's iconic staircase that fanned down to the street. The stairs, beyond repair, were roped off.

My mother's stories of her time at the university were full of contradictions and had an idiosyncratic and improbable logic all their own. Just as there are two stories of creation in Genesis, there were two versions of my mother's time at the University of Havana. In the first, she is the meek young student whose father let her leave the house for class with only enough money for bus fare and a Coca-Cola. In the second, she is the heroine who is determined to get an education at any cost. She is the social work student who went above and beyond expectations, using her own money to get diapers and formula for her clients.

A man who noticed me looking around the campus offered an impromptu tour. He was tall and called himself a mulatto. "There's no racism here like in the United States," he said proudly.

He began his presentation by detailing the events of late 1956. "The university closed down at that time for three years. On March 3, 1957, the president of the university's student body, José Antonio Echevarría, was murdered while storming Batista's presidential palace."

My mother had always referred to Echevarría as "Manzanito"—little apple. The name was a reference to his cheeks that she said were full and red. In her version of history, Batista's henchman gunned down Manzanito only steps away from the famous staircase leading up to the University of Havana. My mother said she was taking a quiz in a nearby classroom when she heard the gunshots.

"Are you sure Echevarría wasn't murdered on campus?" I asked the tour guide.

"Yes, Señora. He died at the presidential palace."

"And classes were suspended in November of 1956?"

"*Claro que sí.*" Of course.

I paused on the word *claro*. Aside from its idiomatic meaning, it was also the word for *clear*. A certain clarity had dawned on me.

"You're sure of the dates?" I asked. By doing the math, I saw that there were five months unaccounted for in my mother's life. The gunshots she said she heard from her classroom in the fall of 1956 never rang out on campus.

"Your mother studied here before she left for America?" he asked.

"She was a student at the School of Social Work. She graduated third in her class."

He looked puzzled. "Señora, there is no School of Social Work here."

"But that's what she told me she studied!"

He looked away.

"She was secretary of the student council and graduated third in her class," I insisted. "She might have ranked higher if she hadn't flunked gym."

"Señora, sometimes Cubanos in exile pass off their stories as the truth."

I thought of my father who always chided that the Cuban exiles he met claimed they had owned sugar plantations. But if my mother hadn't studied social work, what had she studied? Had she attended the university at all? I walked with my new companion in a stunned silence until we came to a small café with a big banner behind the bar that announced the Federación Estudantil Universitaria—the University Student Federation. The man told me Echavarría's story again, and again I felt the sting and the sadness of my mother's lies.

I had never doubted that my mother had a paper trail leading back to a bachelor of arts degree from the University of Havana. I shared her illusions that she had studied at the university. So did the people at Trinity College in Connecticut, who allowed her to make her way into a master's degree program in Spanish literature, based on her claim that her transcripts were trapped behind a rusting iron curtain that clanked shut forever on Cuba. It turned out that her stories about going to the university, her fantasies about graduating at the top of her class, worked as effectively as if she had presented proof of sterling grades. Her stories stood in for academic credits as she bamboozled her way into graduate school. She earned her higher degree in Spanish literature along with a teaching certificate, and was a good teacher despite never having matriculated with a bachelor's degree at the University of Havana, or probably anywhere.

My father should have known that my mother had pulled together a professional life that, like everything she did, was ad hoc. He was a student of history and must have known that her dates didn't align. He also listed in his twenty-fifth Yale reunion book that she was of royal lineage; just as he left her undisturbed when she swayed to a song she hummed, he allowed her to keep her fantastical story of origin.

The man interrupted my thoughts. "Can you give me something in return for my wonderful history lesson?" Everything in Cuba was about bartering. The black market in Havana is darker than Noche Buena, the Christmas Eve sky. People trade anything from sex to American dollars for a pound of meat or a cup of oil. Worried that I didn't understand, the man held out his hand for emphasis, and as I gave him the little cash I had on me, my taxi driver pulled up.

"*Ladrón!*" he yelled as he got out of the car.

The two men faced each other. "It's okay, he can keep the money; it isn't much," I said.

"He stole from you!"

"He showed me some Cuban history," I said, scared and frustrated that the words for landmark or monument were not in my kitchen-Spanish vocabulary.

"*Que cabrón,*" said my driver, calling the man a bastard when we got back in the car. "Don't you know not to go with strange men?"

I knew. But in Havana my curiosity trumped common sense. "I thought you were right behind me," I said apologetically.

We drove on in silence to the Hotel Nacional. As I was getting ready to give my driver the fare, he told me, "I have a mother-in-law in Jersey City who sends my family money whenever she can. It helps more than you can imagine," he said.

I tipped him thirty percent along with half a bottle of Advil.

In Cuba I began to understand how exhausted my parents were from keeping their trastiendas to themselves. Their secrets had once been fairytales that sustained us all, but Aunt Reina told me my mother was never a happy person. "She doesn't smile," she said. I had inherited or perhaps absorbed my mother's melancholia. And yet everything she had told me about life in Cuba was romantic, blessed with ocean breezes.

While so many of my mother's stories were fantasies, my father's stories were ones of omission. I wondered if he had been on a reconnaissance mission to Havana before he met his future wife. Had he ever seen the house on Callé Mercéd with the heavy wood door? Maybe he knocked on it to shake Abuelo's hand on a deal that went awry—his marriage to my mother. Had he seen the four rooms in which my mother lived? Did he know how desperate Abuelo was for American dollars? The story of the ten thousand American dollars still haunted me. As my brother pointed out, in what world would a salesman in a Havana fabric store have access to that kind of foreign currency? Or did he? Was that another one of my mother's stories? Had my brother and I spun our own story out of my mother's tales of make-believe?

My parents' original cream-colored wedding invitation announced that their *ceremonia nupcial* at La Patronato in Havana would happen on December 20, 1959. I went to the address on the invitation: the Jewish Center where the wedding would have taken place. The synagogue was in a building only constructed in the early 1950s; other than the hotel where I was staying, it was among the handful of modern buildings I saw in Cuba. The interior was Sephardic traditional, with a raised bima, or platform, in the middle of the room, and a women's section looking down on the service from the balcony. The sanctuary, with its straight-back, slip-covered chairs gave it the feeling of a dining room. It would have allowed for the formality of my father in a morning coat and a striped cravat, and my mother's long train splayed in the aisle.

Finally, it was time to see Callé Mercéd 20, where my mother grew up, the storied address of my childhood. For me, all things Cuban began and ended there. It was the place where my mother would always be young, where my grandparents shut the door on twenty-five years of possessions and walked away forever. It was the place where my mother said she shined the marble stairs better than the maid. It was my mother's world.

Greenish light painted the façade where I knocked on the heavy door. A pregnant woman answered and invited me inside a small, dark place that almost certainly had not changed since my mother lived there. Maroon brocade furniture crowded the four-room apartment. A big-screen television, the focal point of the living room, broadcast in garish colors and ran without the sound. Like my parents' bedroom on Asylum Avenue, the place felt existentially noisy with so much stuff crammed into such a small space.

The current occupants' furnishings were obviously gifts that their relatives in America brought them since Cuba was once again open for visiting. Their relatives must have taken one of the daily charters to Cuba that left from a corner of Miami's International Airport. Check-in there was a veritable marketplace of American materialism, with Cuban expats emptying Costco and Target and Best Buy goods for their relatives still trapped in Cuba. Carts almost toppled over with boxes of microwaves and televisions. The expats were also determined to get larger items like bicycles, scooters, and air conditioners to their relatives. There was so much concentrated determination in that terminal.

I looked beyond the woman and saw an open-air courtyard between the dining room and the run down kitchen. Courtyards were common in Cuban apartment buildings, and this one was dingy. It was also the place where the *shochet*—the kosher butcher—must have slaughtered the live chickens that my mother said Abuela brought from the marketplace; he cut their throats and drained the blood. As I walked the length of the courtyard, I saw the whitest laundry hanging from a balcony like shiny team pennants. The marble stairs my mother said she had shined were wooden and warped, and led up to a separate second-floor apartment. It was unlikely that my mother's family had occupied both floors, as she claimed; these had always been separate apartments.

My mother once told me that my grandparents sublet the apartment from Abuela's cousin, who was a doctor. Before that, the family lived in a tenement, where they shared a bathroom in the hallway, and prostitutes solicited all night long near my mother's bedroom window. The cousin's office, separate from the rest of the house, was in the back. At one time it was a distinctive, handsomely appointed room with a large mahogany desk shined to a sheen that indicated the doctor's importance. My mother said no one was allowed to go near that space.

I thanked my host profusely and tried to offer her money for the impromptu visit. As soon as I held out the cash I felt like a fat-cat gringa buying memories that weren't quite mine. The only relatives I had left in Cuba were now in graves at the Jewish cemetery in Guanabacoa. She refused the money and sent me on my way with good wishes and blessings.

I couldn't leave yet. I sat on the stoop, my head against the heavy wooden door—the same door my grandfather had quietly pushed open after playing dominoes late into the night. The same door my mother gently tapped on in code to let Abuela know she was home. I finally understood how deeply, how intricately, my mother had invented her comfortable Cubana life until she had believed it herself. There it was again: the story of a life *pegado con chicle*, held together with chewing gum.

While sitting on that stoop, I cried. My tears came as suddenly as a cloudburst, the kind of crying that darkens the mind like a stormy sky. I squeezed my eyes shut and saw a dashboard of pulsing light.

I cried with the recognition that the despairing dances I did with my mother at 1735 Asylum originated here. As a child, I thought my mother missed her grand home in Havana, but the apartment at Callé Mercéd 20 struck me as one of the saddest places in the Cuban capital.

When I returned from the trip, my mother admitted that moving to that apartment in Old Havana had been a step up from her family's previous residence.

Now it was no surprise to me that she had been willing to shed her rich, historic royal name of origin in favor of becoming Mrs. K. Harold Bolton. In Spanish, with its emphasis on the second syllable, the name Bolton had heft. With that Anglicized last name, my mother's family knew she had landed her much-wished-for *Americano fino*—her refined American.

I had parted another sad and rusty iron curtain on a life that my mother never had in her *querida* Cuba. There was no maid, there were no gleaming stairs, there was no second floor with bedrooms or sitting rooms. Instead, this was where my mother secretly pretended to dance with the boys she was not allowed to date—left arm extended, right hand on her stomach. This is the way you dance without a partner, she told me. And once again, I heard her cry out, *Ay Cuba, como te extraño.*

Oh, Cuba, how I miss you.

CHAPTER 24

Prayers and *Trastiendas*

N ow I knew it all—and maybe, still, nothing at all: My father was the dashing spy. My mother was the ultimate survivor.

He never divulged his secrets. She twisted hers into falsehoods. In that way, they both kept their trastiendas. They each lived a lie.

A decade before I was born in 1960, K. Harold Bolton was in the CIA—first under the cover of being an accountant for the United Fruit Company, a well-known CIA front in Guatemala, participating in the 1952 overthrow of the Guatemalan government. He took a stab at destabilizing the Dominican Republic two years later.

My mother—"an emotional terrorist," as I once called her so close to her face that her hot breath suffocated me—invented for herself, and for us, a life of nobility and prestige. These days, she sits confined to a wheelchair in a nearby nursing home, giving Spanish lessons to the residents, who are more advanced in their dementia than she is. I visit twice a week out of a sense of obligation, something I never had to force myself to drum up for my father.

I had been determined to know my father through saying the Kaddish and thought I had failed but, in many ways, it ultimately worked better than all the research and all the interviews and microfiche. I learned early on that saying a daily Kaddish was more than a ritual of mourning. Prayer, it turned out, is more than asking God for favors. It is another channel through which to access memory and create meaning.

My father and the possibilities his story held accompanied me every night of the eleven months I recited those prayers. I not only thought constantly about him, I attempted to will him to come to me, to show me a sign that he was there to help me with my grief. Picture a watercolor in which the features of the person are blurred. The painting elicits a feeling, a spirit, making the person somehow known. That was the way the Kaddish worked. It was through my father the patriot that I became fascinated with reverence, ritual, and protocol, and the Kaddish was the entry and exit to these grieving steps. Everything my father had given me helped me through my grief.

Years after my violin lesson dedicated to silence and after my father died, I searched for the inherent divinity of quietness. I eventually found it in between the very words of the Kaddish prayer. The Kaddish's way of eschewing death, and naming God outright, gives way to a duet of life and death. Yet the prayer, which does not refer to death, brings me into a distinct awareness of God and mourning. For me, the Kaddish was symbolic of a spiritual anechoic chamber in which my public acknowledgment of God's presence harmonized with the private silence of my grief. Even after I had finished the eleven-month ritual, the words of the Kaddish played out in the endless symphony of silence my father had left behind.

On my trip to Havana, I saw the Patronato where my parents' formal wedding was to have taken place. Instead, the wedding happened in a small chapel in the Spanish-Portuguese Synagogue on Central Park West. I took a field trip to see it on a gray January afternoon in 2015.

I rode in a cab against a tide of red brake lights with a driver who claimed he couldn't make change; I gave him twenty dollars for the nine-dollar ride. I had to see the chapel where my mother walked down the aisle in what I envisioned was an absurdly elaborate gown for such a small space. By then, Abuela had painstakingly mended the dress that my mother had shredded with a knife three months earlier, and arrived with it from Cuba the day before the sparsely attended ceremony of

March 26, 1960. It occurred to me that my highly superstitious mother improbably married in a gown that connected her to a stillborn wedding. More twisted luck: The groom drove the bride to the wedding. Abuela sat in the front, shivering in the March cold, while my mother spread out her train in the back seat of my father's shark-finned Chrysler.

"Have you ever heard of such a thing?" my mother once asked me. "A groom bringing a bride to the wedding."

"I have not," I replied solemnly.

The entrance to the synagogue was locked, but through one of the door panes I saw a custodian vacuuming.

"*No puede be here,*" he said, stumbling in the same Spanglish my family spoke. "*Servicio en six-thirty.*"

"*Por favor,*" I pleaded. "*Muy importante. Mis padres se casaron aquí more than fifty years ago.*"

Perhaps the long stretch of time impressed him. He opened the door and motioned for me to put my bag down. I took off my coat and reflexively put my hands up as if I were about to be arrested.

"*Rapido,*" he whispered. And then, in the spirit of participating with me in a reconnaissance mission, he added, "*Buena suerte, Señora.*" Good luck. Mazal.

I hurried around the corner into the plush dark chapel and stopped in the middle of the room at the bima, a small raised platform from which the service is conducted. My parents' huppah, the marriage canopy consisting of four poles to hold up a tallit, or a prayer shawl, would have been adjacent to the bima.

"The prayer shawl belonged to the synagogue," my mother had said, putting forth one of the countless renditions of her wedding day.

The huppah represents the first home a married couple shares. It also connotes the tent in which Abraham and Sarah welcomed visitors passing through their patch of desert. With the tallit doubling as a symbolic roof, this makeshift home has openings on all sides to represent the couple's vulnerability to life's vicissitudes.

As bride and groom, my parents would have faced the chapel's *ner tamid*—the eternal light above the ark. The Ten Commandments in this chapel were etched in gold on whitewashed tablets. This was a traditional synagogue, where men and women sat separately during services: In the style of a Sephardic Jewish synagogue, women sat on the raised benches along the side rather than behind a makeshift wall at the back.

A few people, just ten—barely a minyan—witnessed my parents' marriage. For this wedding, the Boltons had demanded that the small group of men and women sit together. I imagined my Bolton grandmother muttering, "My poor boy," as my grandfather patted her hand. "It's hard to see Harold get married," he would have responded.

"Your grandmother and aunt wore fancy hats and gloves," my mother told me. I can see them with hats perched on coiffed hair, the men in dark suits with pocket squares. Abuela was too cold to take off the coat she had borrowed from my mother's landlady.

I stood in my father's place beneath the huppah where he awaited his bride. I could see him staring at the door to the chapel the way he looked beyond the shiny horizon from the deck of his wartime supply ship—that piercing gaze, or what my aunt inadvertently and inappropriately called "the Asian stare," meaning that the men stationed on ships in the South Pacific stared at the ocean for months at a time. It happened to men like my father whose hopes and dreams lay beyond where the thin blue line of ocean met an illusory land mass. It also happened to my father when he tracked storms at my bedroom window.

I saw my mother enter the chapel, draped in white silk. The train of her gown dwarfed the aisle and a long veil covered her face. The flowers that she bought for herself that morning trembled in her gloved hands. By all accounts, my father had the expression of a dial tone throughout the brief ceremony. "Abuela said she knew widows whose second weddings were more joyous," my mother told me.

I imagine my father shifting his weight and searching his pocket to make sure he has the white gold band to slip on my mother's index finger. He checks inside his jacket for the transliteration of the Hebrew words that Jewish grooms have said to their brides for centuries: *Harei et mekudesht lee b'ta 'ba zi k'dat Moshe v' Yisrael.* Be sanctified to me with this ring in accordance with the laws of Moses and of Israel.

My father steps on a glass, both as a gesture to the ancient destruction of Judaism's temples and a heralding sign of good luck. Do the guests shout mazal tov? There is no reception, no celebratory dinner with family. "*Ni un vaso de agua*," my mother quoted Abuela as saying; the only glass was the one my father broke in accordance with Jewish custom. Did my parents know that their marriage would come to be in shards?

No pictures are taken at the ceremony. They are staged a couple of weeks later at a studio in New Haven, my father in his dark suit with the white hyphen of handkerchief peeking out from his breast pocket. My mother, again in full makeup, including kohl-rimmed eyes, wears the dress whose plunging neckline is held in check by a sparkling brooch. In her white-gloved hands is another cascading bouquet of flowers. In place of her wedding veil she wears an embroidered triangle of cloth that comes to a point with a pearl at the center of her forehead. The effect is of a lacy widow's peak. Her lipstick is unnaturally dark; my father's cheeks are tinted pink.

Harold and Matilde pose in New Haven, Connecticut, for their wedding photograph, taken a week after the March 26, 1960, ceremony.

They do not touch. They do not smile. I have never seen a photograph of them kissing or holding hands. I have never seen them look happy, except briefly when they first reunited in Miami. It was as if my parents had recreated their own stolid version of the wedding picture of my abuelos in Havana.

But where had my father been that summer that I was the human antenna, trying to still Castro's jumpy image in Estersita and Pepé's living room? Where had he been while I uselessly fed dimes into a payphone? He never answered my calls. My mother, bitter, said that he was out playing golf all day and then flirting at the bar with the country club women. I didn't believe her, and I still don't. I'd always had the queasy feeling that, untethered from family, he was off doing something he had always loved more than us. It wasn't golf and it wasn't flirting, and it wasn't in Connecticut.

My brother looked back at that time and guessed that Dad must have been in Chile. "Dad and Felipe might have reunited the summer of 1970 to advise CIA agents about Allende," was his theory. Allende had ruled Chile with an iron fist and had been making too much noise there. Were our childhood visits with Felipe and his family also check-ins between CIA buddies?

The biggest surprise was that one of my mother's paranoid predictions had come true—a young woman had come to our door and my father had looked on her with adoration. There is no doubt in my mind that Ana was his daughter, my half-sister. My attempts to find her wavered among tepidness, terror, and whole-heartedness. Emotions can work that way. If anything, I have been on an emotional journey, which will never have a definitive end. For the moment, it will have to be enough that Ana lives in my heart and my imagination.

I have the same name as a fictional girl detective, and with that mantle I took on the case of my lifetime to find out who exactly my parents were and, by association, who I was. Along the way I discovered a double life for both of them. They told me stories or withheld them. Some of the stories were not true, yet had a spark of truth. I kept them all. Yet I may have burned some of those open-ended stories when I took a match to my father's letter that long-ago summer afternoon. I still see the embossed bald eagle stamp refusing to give in to the flames. I often wonder what, exactly, I burned. Was it a confession? Was it a suicide note? A running list of his past travails that he wrote down like his grocery lists on the shiny cardboard inserts that came with his shirts from the dry cleaner? And did Abuelo ever have the ten thousand American dollars to burn as my mother always claimed?

In this chapel where my parents wed, I stood to say the Kaddish. I wanted those familiar words to help me mourn what was and what could have been for my parents. I wanted to put my difficulties with my parents to rest, and also to release the pull of a mystery that had taken up sprawling real estate in my mind for too long.

It was a lot to ask of a prayer, but I began anyway. Glorified and sanctified is God's name. In that same vein, glorified and sanctified is my father's memory. Glorified and sanctified is my mother's determination to outrun her demons.

Felipe was right: My father was a noble man, my mother a beautiful hysteric. When my mother's time comes, I want the Kaddish to have the spiritual heft, thrust, and drag of an airplane—an airplane she won't be afraid to fly as it carries her soul to heaven.

I recited the full Mourner's Kaddish again. The last words of the prayer rang out in the chapel of the Spanish-Portuguese Synagogue—the place where my parents married, the place where, as the prayer says, I carried the peace that God creates for us all into the future.

ACKNOWLEDGMENTS

So many wonderful people helped shepherd this book into existence. It would not have been a book at all without Jami Bernard. Jami is the extraordinary editor who worked with me for more than a decade to tell the story I needed to tell. Her brilliance, her patience, and her friendship were inextricable parts of the process.

Robert Mandel saw that I had this book in me all along, and generously brought me into the Mandel Vilar fold. Dena Mandel's brilliant, sensitive editing and wise counsel made this book better and deeper. I am so grateful. My agent Heather Jackson's editorial acumen and support contributed immeasurably to the book's publication.

Mary Beth Hinton was a wise and patient copy editor. So much thanks to her. Thank you to Barbara Werden for putting these pages together with care. I am indebted to Sophie Appel for designing the book's beautiful cover.

And then there are my teachers—each one of them has left an imprint on this book and on my soul. My fourth grade teacher, Mrs. Levin, predicted that I would be a writer; I thank her for applauding my book reports. Alan Schwartz taught me to write with commas. Alex Marazano-Lesnevich believed in this book's potential and my ability to write it from its very drafty infancy.

I will be forever grateful that my friend Marcie Hershman invited me to participate in the writers group that she leads with intelligence, wit, and insight. Marcie made a place for me at her table, changing my life for the better as a writer and a person. Leslie Lawrence's dining room was a place of sage writing advice and wonderful friendship. Kim Adrian generously gave me the opportunity to publish my work. Her insights on writing have made me a more careful writer. Howie Axelrod was there with support and excellent critical observations. I thank Richard McCann of blessed memory for inviting me to be part of his wonderful workshop at the Atlantic Center for the Arts.

I worked on significant portions of this book while on fellowships in the quiet beautiful spaces of the Virginia Center for Creative Arts, the Vermont Studio Center, and the Mineral School. Jane Hodges, you are a goddess! The Hadassah-Brandeis Institute generously supported this book in an early incarnation.

I could not have managed without the teachers and students of Grub Street. They are a lifeline to writers. Thank you to Anita Diamant for her steadfast support.

Thank you to Helen Fremont, Stephen McCauley, Gayle Brandeis, Eileen Pollack, Tova Mirvis, and Ruth Behar for their generosity.

I thank Diane Bernard, who guided me through sticky genealogical work. My appreciation and thanks to Kali Foxman and the JewishBoston team, for the time and space to finish the book, and for making my job fun and meaningful. For giving me confidence in this project, I thank Amy Chartock, Michael Chartock, Jill Eskenazi, Becky Franco Friefeld, Avigdor Jacobowitz, Rebecca Kotkin, Deb Milstein, Sandell Morse, Tal Recanati, Jill Segal z'l, and Heather Zacker—all were early, ongoing, and enthusiastic readers.

To Barbara Selmo, my college sister: I wouldn't be me without you.

To Andrea Rossi-Reder, who lived so much of this with me.

"The Bees" of my stellar writing hive have sustained me beyond measure. I send much love to Molly Howes, Shelby Meyerhoff, Meg Senuta, Ann MacDonald, Carroll Sandel, and Katie Bannon. I treasure them all.

The Susans are my beautiful sister-friends in all ways: Susan Silverman inspires me every day and I adore her 6+i; Sue Kahn's humor and love buoy me; and Susan Harris's wisdom and love have made me more perceptive and calmer to the extent that I can be calm! Brenda Goldberg has nourished me in ways too numerous to count. She has seen me, and this book, through many versions, and she still loves me almost as much as I love her! To Miriam Raviv z'l who saved my life and I miss every day. To Bunny and Janet Shapero with much love. Sue Katz Miller believed all along.

My siblings, Carol Bolton Kappel and John Bolton, have lived these stories with me. I love them.

My mother-in-law, Barbara Fasman, has lovingly read my work all these years. She's hoarse from cheering me on!

Without my aunt Raquel Levin, "Uncle Rocks," I would not be who I am. She saved me, and her love means the world to me.

Thank you and love to the extended Fasman family. I send much love to Jonathan Kappel and Dana Kappel. (I told you you'd be in the book, Jonathan!) Love to my Berlowe cousins—Betsy, Jimmy, and Kathy.

My parents will always be towering figures in my life. This is our story in all of its messy glory, complicated emotions, and poignant sadness. There were some funny, quirky moments, too, as well as flashes of joy. Writing about Harold z'l and Matilde all these years has been enlightening and painful. I'm forever grateful that my parents gave me these stories and I hope I told them honestly and well.

And finally to Ken, Anna, and Adam: You are my world. I love you more than I can possibly express. This book and everything I have is for you.

ABOUT THE AUTHOR

Judy Bolton-Fasman grew up in a bilingual home on Asylum Avenue in West Hartford, Connecticut. She attended The Hebrew Academy of Greater Hartford (grades 6 through 9), and in grades 10 through 12, she matriculated in Mount Saint Joseph Academy. She graduated with a BA from Trinity College and earned an MFA from Columbia University.

Judy Bolton-Fasman's essays and reviews have appeared in major newspapers, including the *New York Times* and the *Boston Globe*. She is a frequent contributor to literary magazines such as *McSweeney's, Brevity, Cognoscenti, The Rumpus,* and *Catapult.* Judy Bolton-Fasman is a contributor to the several anthologies including *The Shell Game: Writers Play With Borrowed Forms* and *(Her)oics: Women's Lived Experiences During the Coronavirus Pandemic.*

In addition to receiving a recent Pushcart Prize nomination, Judy is the recipient of the Alonzo G. Davis Fellowship for Latinx writers from the Virginia Center for Creative Arts and has been the Erin Donovan Fellow in Non-Fiction at the Mineral School in Washington. She lives outside of Boston with her family